Hope & Healing for Those with PTSD

Harold G. Koenig, M.D.

ISBN:172445210x
ISBN-13:9781724452108

DEDICATION

To U.S. Veterans and Active Duty Military

CONTENTS

ACKNOWLEDGMENTS

My colleagues Michelle Pearce, Donna Ames, and many others, including VA and military chaplains

INTRODUCTION

Posttraumatic stress disorder (PTSD) is one of the most common and emotionally disabling conditions that humans can experience. PTSD is considered a "disorder" because it interferes with the person's social, occupational, and recreational functioning and destroys quality of life. While this condition is particularly common among those who have served in the military, especially if they have been involved in combat, PTSD is also frequent in the general population. Indeed, if you have PTSD, you are not alone. For example, if you live in the United States, your chances of having an episode of PTSD at some point in your life is about 7% (Koenen et al., 2017). This means that nearly one in 10 will suffer from PTSD (nearly 23 million Americans). In fact, approximately 4% of those in the U.S. have had it within the past year (Kessler et al., 2005). PTSD is also common in other countries besides the U.S. The World Health Organization (WHO) World Mental Health Surveys conducted a survey of 71,083 people in 26 different countries and found that 3.9% met the diagnostic criteria for PTSD at some point in their lives (Koenen et al., 2017). Interestingly, PTSD was more common in the U.S. at 6.9% than it was in Iraq (2.5%), Columbia, South America (2%), or the African continent (2%). Wealth and economic development, then, in no way provide protection from this disorder. People with PTSD often have other psychiatric, social, and medical problems on top of having PTSD and may even be at higher risk for committing suicide. Thus, PTSD is a common and deadly psychiatric disorder that requires treatment. Psychological, pharmacological, and spiritual treatments now exist to help people with PTSD. In this small book, I describe the various treatments for PTSD, many of which have now been shown in scientific studies to help relieve the symptoms of this disorder.

As a psychiatrist, I've found that many of my patients who have experienced severe trauma feel alone sometimes pretty hopeless about their condition, which seems to drag on and on. For that reason, I've written this book specifically for those with PTSD and their families to provide information about this disorder and thereby convey hope that recovery is indeed possible. In fact, more than just recovery, but actual transformation that could never have taken place if the traumatic event or situation had never occurred. I know that seems like a pretty dramatic statement. However, after over 35 years of caring for people with this condition and other emotional problems, I know it is possible.

I will now briefly summarize the content of this book. In Chapter 1, I describe what PTSD is, how it is diagnosed, and what causes it. In Chapter 2, I examine a condition that often occurs together with PTSD called "moral injury," a syndrome that results from a transgression of moral and ethical values that can often occur as part of the trauma or as a result of responses to the trauma. In Chapter 3, I review psychological treatments (psychotherapies) that mental health professionals and clergy often use to treat PTSD and emphasize those shown to be most effective in scientific studies. In Chapter 4, I examine the medical treatments for PTSD including antidepressants and other medications and identify those that are most effective. In Chapter 5, I discussed religious and spiritual approaches to PTSD that you might consider, which have the potential to produce the transformation that I discussed above. In the final

Chapter 6, I summarize the what I said in the previous chapters and make recommendations on what to do if you or a family member suffers from PTSD or the moral injury that often accompanies it. If you are a mental health professional, chaplain, or other clergy, I recommend a book soon to be published titled Religion and Recovery from PTSD written specifically for professional caregivers (Koenig et al., 2019). Please join me now for an information-packed journey on which you will learn a lot about PTSD and what to do about it.

1 **WHAT IS PTSD?**

I begin this book with a brief description of PTSD and how mental health professionals diagnose it. I then describe the various causes of PTSD and characteristics of a person that might help to prevent this disorder after severe trauma.

What is PTSD?

PTSD is a psychiatric disorder that people develop after experiencing a severely stressful event. The stressful event must be a catastrophic one that involves actual or threatened death or injury, or threat to the physical integrity of the person or others through either (1) direct exposure to the trauma (being raped, violently assaulted, or nearly killed), (2) witnessing the trauma happen to someone else, (3) learning about a violent assault, accidental death, rape or unwanted sexual contact of a loved one (family member or intimate partner), or (4) repeatedly being exposed to the results of traumatic events due to one's job or occupation (military, police, firemen, first responders). The event may occur either in childhood or adulthood. These are the criteria listed in the Diagnostic and Statistical Manual of Mental Disorders, 5th Edition [DSM-5] (American Psychological Association, 2013).

Psychiatrists will diagnose PTSD when such a traumatic stressor is present and is followed by symptoms in all of the following four categories: (1) intrusions (recurrent, involuntary memories, nightmares, flashbacks); (2) avoidance (persistent efforts to avoid trauma-related thoughts, feelings, or external reminders such as people, activities, situations, smells, sounds, places, movies, etc.); (3) negative moods or thoughts associated with the trauma (persistent negative beliefs and expectations of oneself or others, fear, anger, guilt, shame, decreased interest, detachment, difficulty experiencing emotions such as love and care for others); and (4) changes in arousal or reactivity (irritable, aggressive, self-destructive, hypervigilant, easily startled, difficulties concentrating, difficulty sleeping). One or two symptoms in each of these four categories is required for the diagnosis of PTSD. Symptoms related to the trauma must (a) last for a least one month (immediately after the trauma or may emerge months or years after the trauma); (b) cause significant distress or problems with social, occupational or recreational functioning; and (c) cannot be the result of medication, substance use or other psychiatric illness that might better explain the symptoms.

Many other psychiatric conditions, however, often occur right along with PTSD that may be difficult to distinguish from PTSD itself. These include depression, panic disorder, obsessive-compulsive disorder, antisocial personality disorders, and alcohol or drug use disorders. These conditions may have been present prior to the onset of PTSD (increasing vulnerability to it) or may follow after it (as a reaction to the distressing symptoms of PTSD). Social problems are also frequent such as marital conflict, spousal abuse, divorce, and alienation from children, friends, associates or coworkers. PTSD is truly a devastating disorder that destroys life for the person and those around him or her. Not surprisingly, suicidal thoughts and attempts are common in those with PTSD and increase with each additional traumatic event that the person experiences (LeBouthillier et al., 2015).

What causes PTSD?
According to the WHO World Mental Health Surveys, nearly

three-quarters (70%) of people around the world report having experienced a severe traumatic stressor at some point in their lives and often more than just one (on average, people in this survey reported 3.2 such traumatic stressors) (Kessler et al., 2017). Among those reporting traumatic stressors (in other words, 7 of 10 people), only 5.6% developed PTSD (Koenen et al., 2017). This means that the most (94%) of those who experience a traumatic stressor that seriously threatens their own life or the lives of their loved ones do not develop PTSD. Why is that the case?

No doubt, the type of stressor determines in part the likelihood that a person will experience PTSD. The highest risk of PTSD is found in those who are raped (19%), physically abused by an intimate partner (12%), kidnapped (11%), or sexually assaulted other than rape (11%). The risk is much lower in other categories of trauma (2-5%) (Kessler et al., 2017). Nearly one-quarter (23%) of U.S. Veterans who participated in Operation Enduring Freedom or Operation Iraqi Freedom were diagnosed with PTSD in one study (Fulton et al., 2015). Studies have also shown that PTSD may emerge many years after the trauma. The initial trauma may make a person more vulnerable to future traumas, even if they are less severe than the original one. In addition, disabling physical health problems that prevent a person from staying busy with job, hobbies, or family activities. Some people, however, are simply more vulnerable to PTSD than are others.

Individuals at greater risk for PTSD are women (who may be more emotionally sensitive to trauma), those in middle-age (with multiple other responsibilities), persons with low education or IQ (fewer intellectual resources to cognitively deal with the trauma), ethnic minorities (more stressful life events in general), the socially disadvantaged, those with lower household income or unemployed (fewer resources in general to deal with the trauma), those with non-straight sexual orientation (high life stress due to discrimination and social ostracism), and persons with other current psychological problems or a history of anxious/depressed childhood temperament. One of the strongest risk factors PTSD is experience of childhood deprivation or abuse (called "adverse childhood experiences"). In addition, as noted earlier, prior trauma exposure of any kind (multiple life stressors) increases vulnerability to PTSD.

Among military personnel, risk factors for PTSD are involvement in combat, discharging a weapon (killing enemy combatants), witnessing someone wounded or killed, lower military rank, being in the Army, having a high number of deployments, longer cumulative length of deployments, marital status (unmarried), and younger age (less emotional and intellectual maturity at the time of the trauma).

As noted above, physical health problems may reactivate PTSD. However, sudden onset of life-threatening medical illness may also directly cause it. For example, one recent study found that 6 to 14 percent of patients develop PTSD after being diagnosed with cancer (Cordova et al., 2017). Admission to and treatment in the intensive care unit (ICU) may also result in a host of PTSD symptoms (e.g., avoidance of medical clinics or hospitals, obsessive concerns about recurrence of illness, hypervigilance for physical symptoms, fear of contracting illness, claustrophobia due to physical restraint during the ICU stay, avoidance of news about medical topics, or exaggerated startle responses when hearing beeping noises like those encountered in the ICU).

Prevention of PTSD

There are also certain characteristics, attitudes and behaviors that may protect a person from developing PTSD after severe trauma or speed recovery once PTSD develops. As noted above, psychological stability prior to the onset of severe trauma (i.e., absence of depression, anxiety, personality disorder, prior trauma) may help to prevent PTSD, depending on the severity of the trauma. However, if the trauma is severe enough (e.g., prolonged torture and threat of death), anyone -- no matter how healthy they are -- can develop the disorder. Adequate social and family support is a major factor that helps to both prevent the onset of PTSD and increases speed of recovery.

Another characteristic, one that is often ignored by mental health professionals, is religious/spiritual belief and support from a faith community. The evidence for this is not only the many, many testimonials of those suffering severe trauma, but also considerable research (see Koenig et al., 2019, for a detailed description of these studies). For example, greater intrinsic religiosity (devout, internalized religious commitment) is related to lower PTSD symptoms among youth exposed to terrorism, and this is also true for adults exposed to many other types of trauma. One study of teachers from El Salvador who were exposed to gang violence found that daily spiritual experiences were inversely related to PTSD symptoms and positively related to deriving meaning from the trauma and growing from the traumatic experience (Kurian et al., 2016). Likewise, in a study of 890 persons during the three years following the September 11th terrorist attacks in New York City, McIntosh et al (2011) found that higher intrinsic religiosity at the time of the trauma protected individuals from developing future PTSD symptoms.

The benefits of religious involvement are not limited to civilians. A growing amount of research is showing that religious involvement may help to prevent PTSD among members of our military as well. For example, in a study of 3,543 women U.S. Veterans (VA Women's Health Project), those who were sexually assaulted during their time in the military reported more depressive symptoms and worse mental health (Chang et al., 2001). However, among those who attended religious services more frequently, depressive symptoms were significantly lower and mental health significantly better; similar findings were reported in a study of male Veterans suffering from sexual assault in the military (Chang et al., 2003). More recently, surveys of US Veterans have reported that religious attendance and private religious activities were lower among those with PTSD compared to those without. Similar findings (particularly for private religious activities such as prayer) were reported by Tait et al (2016) in a study of Veterans recently returning from deployment to Iraq or Afghanistan. These studies suggest that those who are more actively involved in religious or spiritual activities experience fewer PTSD symptoms.

Now, to be honest, there are several possible reasons for these findings. Not only may religious involvement prevent the onset of PTSD, PTSD may also adversely affect a person's religious beliefs and activities. The experience of severe trauma may disrupt a person's worldview and belief that a loving God exists and protects them from harm. There are many good and deeply religious people who in difficult situations have prayed for help or protection, and yet have been severely traumatized by the occurrence of adverse events despite those prayers. This is common among members of the military or those who have been raped or sexually violated. How does one make sense of such experiences? It is not surprising, then, that religious struggles are common among those with PTSD (see next chapter).

Nevertheless, there is little doubt that religious or spiritual involvement does help some persons with PTSD recover more quickly from their disorder, if they can maintain that involvement after the trauma. In one of the best and most comprehensive studies to date, researchers examined religious/spiritual involvement in 532 U.S. Veterans with severe combat-related PTSD requiring admission to a 60- to 90-day residential treatment program (Currier et al., 2015). Religious and spiritual activities and experiences and PTSD symptoms were assessed shortly after admission to the program and then again at the time of program discharge. Those who were more engaged in religious and spiritual practices on entry into the program, despite their severe PTSD symptoms, experienced a faster relief of symptoms during their 60 to 90 day stay in the treatment program.

Conclusions

PTSD is a psychiatric disorder characterized by a set of symptoms that have persisted for at least one month (and often much longer) following a severe traumatic stressor. There are many causes for PTSD, including the type and severity of the traumatic stressor, certain personal characteristics (gender, age, marital status, etc.), and prior history of psychological problems, childhood trauma, or multiple stressful life events (including life-threatening medical illness). There are also factors that may help to prevent the onset of PTSD after severe stress, including adequate social and family support, strong intrinsic religious beliefs, private religious practices such as prayer and meditation (when engaged in regularly prior to the stressor), and active involvement in a faith community that can provide support both during and after trauma or loss. There is also evidence that religious and spiritual beliefs/practices can help speed recovery from PTSD, even when the disorder is severe and long-lasting. These findings provide a scientific basis for psychological treatments described in Chapter 3 and religious/spiritual treatments as described in Chapter 5.

Bear in mind, however, the severe traumatic stress can also influence a person's religious/spiritual beliefs and practices, causing religious struggles and sometimes even a complete loss of religious faith. This is a type of moral injury, which I will examine more closely in the next chapter.

2 MORAL INJURY AND PTSD

Moral injury is a syndrome that often accompanies PTSD, and yet is quite distinct from it. Moral injury may occur in the absence of PTSD (just as PTSD can occur in the absence of moral injury). The reason moral injury is so important when it occurs in those with PTSD is that it can interfere with recovery from PTSD unless adequately addressed. While psychological therapies have been attempted in the treatment of moral injury in the setting of PTSD, spiritual or religious approaches may be more appropriate and potentially more effective. In this chapter, I will define moral injury and examine how common it is among those with PTSD. In Chapter 5, when describing religious and spiritual treatments for PTSD, I will return to the topic of moral injury and describe various approaches that can be taken to treat it.

Definition
What is moral injury (sometimes also called "inner conflict")? There are many definitions for this term, although the one I like the best (at least as it applies to military personnel) is:

> [Moral injury reflects] the deleterious effects of war participation [or other severe trauma] on moral conscience and ethical conceptions – the wrecking of a

> person's fundamental assumptions about 'what's right' and how things should work in the world that may result from a sense of having violated one's core moral identity and lost any reliable, meaningful world in which to live…moral injury involves acts of moral compromise or the violation of values and beliefs (by oneself or others) that potentially threaten soldiers' ability to admire or even recognize themselves or trust in the reality of others in the world (Kelle, 2017, p 94).

While this definition refers specifically to members of the military, simply changing a few words in the definition could make it easily applicable to civilians in the context of severe traumatic stress.

Moral injury is a syndrome that consists of both psychological religious/spiritual (R/S) aspects (Koenig, 2018a). The psychological dimension involves symptoms such as feeling of guilty, shame, feelings of betrayal by others, concerns over transgression of moral values, loss of trust in others, loss of meaning and purpose in life, difficulty forgiving others and self, and condemning oneself over actions or inaction. The R/S dimension involves religious or spiritual struggles (including difficulty forgiving God) and a weakening or loss of religious faith. The R/S aspects of moral injury are often ignored by mental health professionals, but it is a crucial aspect of the internal conflict that many feel after transgressing moral standards or values. Helping individuals with moral injury deal with R/S issues like this is squarely in the province of trained clergy, particularly chaplains and pastoral counselors with experience helping those with PTSD.

Although moral injury often occurs in the setting of PTSD, as noted above, it is a syndrome separate and distinct from PTSD. Recall from the last chapter that PTSD involves intrusive symptom (nightmares and flashbacks), avoidance behaviors (avoiding internal or external reminders of the trauma), negative emotions (amnesia concerning the traumatic event, negative beliefs, exaggerated blame, negative emotions, loss of interest, social withdrawal), and hypervigilance (irritable, aggressive, increased startle response, trouble concentrating). These symptoms are very different from those of moral injury described earlier. If there is any overlap, it is in the PTSD Criterion D symptom cluster (negative thoughts and emotions).

Moral injury can also occur in the absence of severe traumatic stress. Transgressions of one's moral code and values occur all the time and in almost every situation. Indeed, the Scriptures of both Judaism and Christianity emphasize this very point: "Indeed, there is no one on earth who is righteous, no one who does what is right and never sins" (Ecclesiastes 7:20) and "…all have sinned and fall short of the glory of God" (Romans 3:23).

Is Moral Injury Common?

How common is moral injury (MI) in the setting of PTSD? The answer is *very* common. Our research in military personnel found the following. Among active duty US military personnel, over 80% with PTSD symptoms have at least one symptom of MI of high severity (i.e., rated the symptom a 9 or 10 on a severity scale from 1 to 10) and 52% had four or more MI symptoms at this severity level (Volk & Koenig, 2018). U.S. Veterans are even more likely to report MI symptoms. For example, in a multi-site survey of Veterans with PTSD symptoms from across the United States, we found that over 90% rated at least one MI symptom a 9 or 10 on a 1 to 10 severity scale and 59% indicated five or more MI symptoms at this severity level (Koenig et al., 2018a).

Consequences of Moral Injury

MI is in no way a benign condition. First, MI is strongly correlated with PTSD severity. Therefore, the more severe the PTSD symptoms are, the more likely that MI is also present, leaving open the possibility that MI may be either worsening PTSD symptoms or PTSD symptoms are worsening MI.

Indeed, MI can make PTSD symptoms worse and vice versa, creating a downward vicious cycle. Second, MI may interfere with the treatment of PTSD, such that psychotherapy or medication is less effective in those with MI and PTSD, resulting in repeated clinic visits and continuing symptoms for months or even years. This has been shown to be especially true among Veterans who experience a loss of religious faith as a result of their wartime experiences (Fontana & Rosenheck, 2004).

Third, given the severe emotional pain and inner conflict that MI causes, those with this syndrome are more likely to have suicidal thoughts and exhibit suicidal behaviors, even after accounting for PTSD severity and depression. MI by itself, then, may drive a person to commit suicide. People with severe MI may prefer to die rather than continue to experience inner psychological and spiritual struggles that seem to be causing endless pain that they cannot stop.

Finally, the enormous suffering that MI causes can dramatically affect a person's quality of life, ability to function on the job, and relationships with friends and family members. Imagine what it must be like to feel guilty and ashamed all the time, constantly ruminating over past actions that can never be undone. Or feeling that one has been betrayed by close friends, superiors, or family members on whom one depended for guidance, protection and sustenance (childhood abuse or trauma). Or feeling like one has done something wrong and unable to resolve those feelings. Or losing trust in other people, fearful that they will let you down or not be available when you really need them. Or losing all meaning and purpose in life, simply living day-to-day without a sense of direction. Or feeling resentful and angry at what others have done to you, trapped in the prison of unforgiveness. Or condemning yourself over and over again for whatever you did or didn't do, punishing yourself for real or imagined crimes. Or feeling that God is punishing you, persecuting you, or is distant and unable to help, or that your faith community has deserted you. Or maybe losing your faith entirely, unable to pray or receive comfort from your religious beliefs. Now, add to that the symptoms of PTSD -- sudden flashbacks of the traumatic experience occurring in the middle of the day, terrifying nightmares that disrupt your sleep, unable to watch television programs or engage in intimate relationships that remind you of the trauma, and startled or enraged at the least provocation. Indeed, no need to wait for hell after you die, because you are in it now. But why continue like this, when there are both psychological, medical, and especially, religious solutions -- those that have proven to be effective over thousands of years.

Conclusion

Moral injury is a syndrome that is distinct from PTSD, but it is very common among those who experience severe trauma or loss, either as a result of the trauma itself or a result of behaviors (moral transgressions) following the trauma. The consequences of moral injury are serious and may worsen PTSD symptoms, interfere with the treatment of PTSD, destroyed quality of life, and even lead to suicide, underscoring the need to treat this condition – right along with the PTSD that often accompanies it. The next chapter examines what can be done to help those suffering from PTSD, when occurring with or without MI.

3 THE TALKING CURE

It was Sigmund Freud nearly 100 years ago who came up with the term "the talking cure." Although he was referring to psychoanalysis when he initially use the term, talking about one's problems in a safe environment with someone who is trusted, has long been shown to help with the resolution of loss, trauma, and other emotional problems.

I begin now a discussion of treatments for PTSD, starting first with a review of standard secular psychotherapies that are now commonly used to treat this disorder. Mental health professionals who provide these treatments typically have advanced degrees, are licensed by the state, and received special training to administer the particular type of psychotherapy being offered. You may be surprised that current guidelines for the treatment of PTSD recommend psychotherapy over medication and all other treatments. This is based on a large volume of research showing that the benefits from psychotherapy in PTSD far exceed those of medications (and are without the side effects that medications have). Furthermore, the benefits of psychotherapy are more long-lasting than those of medication, which may help some persons only during the time that the medication is actually being taken. If you want to know more details about the various psychotherapies discussed in this chapter, my colleagues and I have written a more comprehensive and detailed review of the effects of different forms of psychotherapy in PTSD (Koenig et al., 2019).

Many different kinds of psychotherapies have been proposed for the treatment of PTSD. However, only a few of these have been shown in scientific studies (i.e., randomized clinical trials) to have benefit. I will now discuss each of these below, as well as other psychological approaches to treatment that are reasonable but have far less evidence to support their effectiveness. When discussing these various psychotherapies and psychological treatments (along with medications in Chapter 4), I will be referring to what is called an "effect size" (ES). The ES indicates the size of the clinically meaningful effect that the treatment has. In other words, the ES is a quantitative measure of the benefits that you may receive after undergoing a course of the particular type of psychotherapy discussed below. ES's that indicate a small clinical effect on reducing PTSD symptoms are those that are -0.20 or closer to 0; a moderate effect is indicated by ES's in the range of -0.30 to -0.60; and a large clinical effect or benefit is indicated by ES's in the -0.80 or more negative range. ES's also have what are called "95% confidence intervals." This is a statistical term that means 95% of people who received the therapy fall within the range of values provided. If a 95% confidence interval includes 0, then the clinical benefit of the treatment is considered to be the same as no treatment at all.

Most of the time these studies compare the psychotherapy being studied with a "control" condition where participants receive no treatment (controls might be placed on waitlist to receive the therapy later or may simply receive "usual care," i.e., the care they would ordinarily receive if they were not in the study). On occasion, the psychotherapy being studied will be compared with another "active" treatment (such as another type of psychological treatment or medication). Of course, it is much more difficult to show a large ES (indicating a clinically meaningful difference) if a psychotherapy is compared to another treatment than if it is compared to no treatment or usual care.

Now that may be more information that you are interested in, but it may be helpful so that we can compare the effects of psychotherapy with medication and other treatments.

Psychotherapies currently used to treat PTSD can be divided into "trauma-focused therapies" and "non-trauma-focused therapies." I begin with the trauma-focused therapies, since these are usually recommended for those with PTSD.

Trauma-Focused Therapies

The US Department of Veterans Affairs (VA) and Department of Defense (DoD), as well as the American Psychological Association (APA), recommend either Prolonged Exposure or Cognitive Processing Therapy as first-line treatments for PTSD. Again, these guidelines all recommend these psychotherapies above other psychological approaches and above medication (VA/DoD, 2017; APA, 2017). In fact, the VA now requires that these two psychotherapies be made available to all Veterans with PTSD.

Prolonged Exposure (PE). One of the "symptom clusters" necessary to have a diagnosis of PTSD (as noted in Chapter 1) is avoidance of memories, people, places, sounds, or situations that remind a person of the traumatic event. Because of the severe distress caused by reminders of the traumatic event, those with PTSD do everything possible to avoid them. They purposefully try to suppress any memory of the event by avoiding talking about it, shy away from situations or people that remind them of what happened, and avoid places that bring back the feelings they experienced at the time of the trauma. Unfortunately, while avoiding reminders of the traumatic experience help the person to feel better in the short term, in the long-term avoidance reinforces PTSD symptoms and makes them even worse. As a result, memories of the trauma "pop" back into consciousness in the form of flashbacks (sudden experiences of the trauma as if it were happening in the present), nightmares of the event that disrupt sleep, and many of the other symptoms characteristic of PTSD.

Therefore, the core treatment in PE is gradual conscious exposure of the person to memories and other aspects of the traumatic event that they are trying to avoid (Foa et al., 2008). This is based on a psychological rationale called Emotional Processing Theory. This theory argues, based on plenty of scientific evidence, that repeatedly exposing a person to events or situations that cause anxiety leads to what is called "habituation" of the fear (basically, you get used to it). This results in a decrease in the anxiety associated with the memory of the event that is called "extinction." This is the same principle behind the treatment of people who have phobias (fear of heights, fear of spiders, fear of closed-end spaces, etc.), i.e., exposure to the very situation that causes intense fear. Such exposure is done very gradually and with much support in a safe environment.

Understandably, PE is not a treatment the timid or unmotivated. This treatment – while very effective – takes a considerable amount of courage and effort. As a result, PE is often administered together with other psychological techniques that reduce anxiety and produce relaxation immediately prior to and during the exposure. Furthermore, there are several types of exposure to traumatic memories that are implemented during PE, which cause different levels of anxiety.

The three ways of exposing a person to traumatic memories are imaginal exposure, in vivo exposure, and virtual reality exposure. I will discuss each of these here. During *imaginal exposure*, the person -- while sitting in the safety of the therapist's office -- is asked to imagine events, situations, sounds, and feelings they experienced during the traumatic event. The person describes events and feelings out loud to the therapist during the session. This is done repeatedly during 60- to 90-minute sessions conducted weekly over a period of 12 weeks (on average). When anxiety becomes too high, the therapist brings the person out of their imagination and grounds them in the present, often using relaxation techniques.

Imaginal exposure is often combined with *in vivo exposure*

where the therapist and client work together to identify a list of experiences and situations similar to the traumatic event (from least to most anxiety provoking). The person is then encouraged to participate in real life in the previously avoided situations/activities on the list. The therapist may initially accompany the person during these in vivo activities, but as anxiety lessons, the individual will be asked to do them on their own.

Finally, *virtual reality exposure* is a form of imaginal exposure that simulates in-vivo exposure without placing the person at risk of harm that would otherwise occur if exposed to the real situation. A variety of software programs have been developed to produce a replication of the traumatic event with dramatic visual and real-life sound effects. For example, the software program *Bravemind* simulates a situation in Iraq/Afghanistan using 3D graphics along with smells, vibrations and sounds like those experienced during combat (Rizzo & Shilling, 2018).

The average effect size for all different kinds of PE is large, ranging from -1.08 to -2.32.   Recall that ES's above -0.80 are considered large. So for those who are brave, this treatment really works. The ES's above involve the average effect of many randomized clinical trials involving hundreds of individuals with PTSD. As noted earlier, PE is often administered together with relaxation techniques (slow deep breathing, progressive, muscle relaxation, meditation, etc.) to help reduce the anxiety that the exposure arouses.

If a person has difficulty expressing their memories and feelings out loud to their therapist (as required during imaginal exposure), and alternative treatment is Written Exposure Therapy (WET). WET, as the name implies, involves writing about the trauma, which is done repeatedly while guided and supported by the therapist. This treatment typically involves five or six 30-minute sessions. It is unclear whether WET is as effective as standard PE, although a recent study found that five 30-minute sessions of WET were as effective as twelve 60-minute sessions of cognitive processing therapy (Sloan et al.,

2018). These findings, however, need to be replicated (since they seem almost too good to be true and the study methodology has been criticized by trauma experts).

Eye Movement Desensitization and Reprocessing (EMDR) involves having the person recall/imagine memories, situations, and feelings of a traumatic event (imaginal exposure) at the same times as the therapist induces a series of side-to-side eye movements or hand tapping. The person is asked to imagine the worst part of their trauma and to think of a negative thought about the trauma allowing for negative emotions to emerge, while at the same time following movement of the therapist's fingers from side-to-side. The client then reports their experiences to the therapist. This is done repeatedly throughout the session.

EMDR has gotten a lot of public press recently and has been particularly trendy among PTSD therapists. However, EMDR has been found to be only moderately effective in the treatment of PTSD (average ES=-0.66, 95% CI=-.44 to -0.89, based on 22 studies in one review), the reduction in PTSD symptoms is not as large as found in standard PE. In fact, some trauma experts claim that the eye and hand movements in EMDR are simply distractions and the real therapeutic element is the exposure to traumatic memories and emotions that is included in the treatment.

Cognitive Processing Therapy (CPT). CPT is considered to be a cousin of cognitive behavioral therapy (CBT), a treatment that has been used widely for the treatment of depression, anxiety, and many other emotional disorders, and found to be very effective in literally hundreds of randomized clinical trials. CBT is a form of psychotherapy that challenges a person's beliefs and behaviors that are causing or worsening their emotional symptoms. CPT is a variant of CBT, where the therapist teaches the person (or client) to identify trauma-related negative thoughts about themselves or others and then change them. Clients are taught to identify, label, and separate events, thoughts, and emotions from each other, which commonly tend to be lumped together by those with PTSD. Unrealistic or distorted thoughts are challenged, unhealthy behaviors discouraged, and healthy behaviors encouraged, all within a supportive atmosphere. Clients may be asked to write a detailed account of the trauma (the trauma narrative), and so CPT may involve some level of trauma exposure. Clients are given homework sessions to complete between sessions. The treatment is administered in twelve 60-minute sessions that are delivered once or twice per week over a period of 6 to 12 weeks.

CPT was originally developed about 20 years ago by psychologist Patricia Resick for rape victims, although has been widely studied and used to treat Veterans and active duty military personnel with PTSD. CPT may also be administered as a group intervention, although may not be as effective as individual one-on-one therapy. CPT by video-teleconferencing (VTC) has also been shown to be effective in the treatment of PTSD with results similar to that for in-person CPT. A version of CPT has been developed (called CPT-C) that excludes the trauma narrative, thereby reducing the anxiety associated with trauma exposure. CPT-C has been shown to be as effective as standard CPT (with the trauma neck narrative). Thus, only CPT-C (cognitive version) is now recommended (Resick et al., 2017).

Within the last 20 years, CPT has been shown to be effective in the treatment of female rape victims, US veterans, and active duty military with PTSD. Based on multiple meta-analyses of randomized clinical trials published in the literature, the average ES for CPT (typically compared to controls on a waitlist or those receiving no treatment) ranges from -0.89 to -1.69. Thus, the effectiveness of CPT is similar to that of PE. In studies that have directly compared PE and CPT, most report similar benefits from the therapy, although CPT may be more effective than PE in Veterans (Haagen et al., 2015).

<u>Other Psychotherapies and Psychological Approaches</u>. As noted above, many other psychological treatments have been

proposed for the treatment of PTSD. These treatments are often focused on a particular subgroup. They include *Cognitive Trauma Therapy for Battered Women* for those who have been separated from their abusers and are now living independently; *Helping to Overcome PTSD through Empowerment* for women who are currently living in shelter and have multiple resource needs; *Dialectical-Behavior Therapy-Prolonged Exposure* for those with PTSD and borderline personality disorder; *Brief Eclectic Psychotherapy* (BEP), a form of psychodynamic therapy that tries to relate early childhood experiences to emotional reactions to trauma experienced during adulthood; and *Stress Inoculation Training.* Stress Inoculation Training involves learning skills to manage trauma-related anxiety such as progressive deep muscle relaxation, cue-controlled and differential relaxation, thought stopping, positive self-dialogue, cognitive restructuring, guided modeling, and role-playing. Research demonstrating the effectiveness of all these treatment approaches is weaker than for either PE or CPT, and therefore they are generally not recommended (with some exceptions, such as battered women). For more details on these therapies see Koenig et al. (2019).

Therapies Not Focusing on the Trauma

A wide range of therapies have been used to treat PTSD that do not specifically focus on the traumatic event, but rather on symptoms such as depression, anxiety, or other negative emotions and behaviors. Even though these treatments may be less anxiety producing, multiple reviews of the research on non-trauma-focused therapies have concluded that these treatments are not as effective as those that focus on the trauma itself. Examples of such treatments include non-trauma-focused CBT, psychodynamic and interpersonal psychotherapies, supportive therapy, and general stress management skills such as deep abdominal breathing and muscle relaxation.

Other psychological approaches suggested for PTSD including Acceptance and Commitment Therapy (ACT); various integrative therapies such as tai chi, yoga, or secular meditation;

employment therapy and other efforts to help reintegrate those with PTSD back into the community through volunteering, attending school, etc. These have been particularly helpful for Veterans involved in a recovery model now being promoted by many VA treatment facilities.

Conclusions

Trauma-focused psychotherapies, particularly Prolonged Exposure and Cognitive Processing Therapy, are the most effect and commonly recommended treatments for PTSD, endorsed by both military bodies (Department of Defense and Veterans Administration) and the American Psychological Association in their consensus guidelines. These therapies have large treatment effects that are clinically meaningful. However, despite these benefits, few persons with PTSD actually complete these therapies, and even of those who complete therapy, more than 50% are left with significant residual symptoms of PTSD (Koenig et al., 2019). There is much room, then, for novel trauma-focused treatments for this disorder that achieve greater symptom reduction and remission of symptoms. I will next look at the contribution to symptom relief that medications can make.

4 CAN MEDICATION HELP?

Medicines have long been prescribed for the treatment of PTSD, although as noted in the last chapter, drug treatment is not as effective as trauma-focused psychotherapies in persons with this disorder. I will review here the different medications used to treat PTSD and their effectiveness based on meta-analyses[1] of randomized clinical trials. While medication is not considered a first-line treatment for PTSD, it may sometimes be necessary to relieve symptoms to the point that people are able and willing to engage in trauma-focused psychotherapies.

Case Vignette
>Richard is a 25-year old married male serving in the U.S. Army and stationed in Afghanistan. This is his third deployment to the region, and while the first two deployments went well, the present one had been very difficult. Shortly after arriving in Kabul, his armored personnel carrier drove over an IED (improvised explosive device) killing a close buddy from his previous tours riding with him and severely wounding another

---

[1] A meta-analysis is a compilation of dozens and sometimes hundreds of randomized clinical trials involving thousands of patients, where results are averaged to determine an average effect size and 95% confidence interval across all studies.

member of his team (leg severely crushed, likely needing amputation). Richard suffered a mild closed head injury from the blast but was alert enough after he awoke to realize the carnage around him. Shaken by this experience, he began experiencing frequent flashbacks of the explosion during the day and nightmares where he saw the faces and wounded bodies of his comrades. Unable to continue his duties over the next two months, he was evaluated by behavioral health, who diagnosed him with PTSD. As a result, Richard was sent back home to the U.S. to recover. Since this was his third and last deployment and he was ending the period of his enlistment, plans were made for his discharge from the military. His PTSD symptoms, however, persisted after returning home affecting his ability to work and interfering with his family relationships. At his wife's encouragement, Richard scheduled an appointment at the local Veterans Affairs hospital for treatment. The psychologist who evaluated him at the VA confirmed the diagnosis of PTSD and recommended Prolonged Exposure Therapy (PET). After hearing about what this would entail, Richard refused. He could not imagine reliving the horrific experiences he had gone through in Afghanistan. The psychologist recommended he also see a psychiatrist, who after evaluating him, recommended a trial of paroxetine (trade name Paxil). Richard agreed and started the treatment. After four weeks, he noticed that his hyperarousal, anxiety and intrusive flashbacks were somewhat better, as was his sleep. The psychiatrist recommended he reconsider therapy with the psychologist. Now that he was feeling a bit better, Richard agreed and began a 3-month treatment program of weekly PET.

The reader is now warned. The following review will get pretty dense as I describe the medications used to treat PTSD and the research that has examined their effectiveness. However, this review is probably the most recent and comprehensive systematic review that exists today (July 2018) of drug treatments for PTSD. Not all readers will be interested in the detailed information presented in this chapter; however, for those wanting an updated review on this topic, there is probably no better one (in this author's humble opinion). Again, the effect size (ES) is an important issue here, since we can compare this metric with the ES's achieved by psychotherapies discussed in the last chapter.

I now review the various classes of medications used to treat PTSD (not all of which are recommended by current guidelines). These include antidepressants, anticonvulsants, antipsychotics, benzodiazepines, α1 adrenergic antagonists, glutaminergic agonists, and other somatic therapies (**Table 4.1**).

Antidepressants

The only medications for PTSD (and only if trauma-focused psychotherapies are not available or not preferred) currently recommended by the U.S. Food and Drug Administration are paroxetine and sertraline (i.e., serotonin reuptake inhibitors). These recommendations are now almost 10 years old (Stein et al., 2009). The American Psychological Association and Veterans Affairs/Department of Defense treatment guidelines have broadened the range of medications now recommended for PTSD to include paroxetine, sertraline, fluoxetine, and venlafaxine for the treatment of PTSD (and only these four medications).

Serotonin Reuptake Inhibitors (SSRIs). SSRIs inhibit the reuptake of serotonin in the space between neurons in the brain making it more available for neuronal transmission. Defects in serotonin are thought to play an important part in the physiological abnormalities found in PTSD. In three meta-analyses involving more than 20 studies in over 3,000 patients, SSRI's overall have an ES ranging from -.23 to -.48, which indicates a small to moderate clinical effect (Watts et al., 2013;

Hoskins et al., 2015; Lee et al., 2016). For individual SSRI's the ES of sertraline (Zoloft) ranges from -.13 to -.51 (again, small to moderate); for paroxetine (Paxil), the ES ranges from -.36 to -.74 (moderate); the ES of fluoxetine (Prozac) ranges from -.23 to -.43 (small to moderate); and for citalopram (Celexa), the range is +.13 to +.74 (this medication actually causes worse symptoms compared to placebo!). Note that SSRIs are the most commonly prescribed antidepressant for the treatment of Veterans with PTSD in Veterans Affairs (VA) hospitals and clinics (Bernardy et al., 2012). However, the ESs for SSRI's are dwarfed by those of trauma-focused psychotherapies that are typically -1.00 or larger, which is the basis for current recommendations.

Serotonin-Norepinephrine Reuptake Inhibitors (SNRIs). Of the two main SNRIs, venlafaxine (Effexor) and duloxetine (Cymbalta), only venlafaxine has been examined in a randomized clinical trial examining its efficacy in PTSD. Although there was an initial case report that PTSD symptom were made worse by duloxetine (Deneys & Ahearn, 2006), research since then has largely dispelled such concerns based on at least two 8-12-week open label/naturalistic trials whose results were quite promising (Villareal et al., 2010; Walderhaug et al., 2010). With regard to venlafaxine, Watts et al (2013) and Hoskins et al (2015) reported small to moderate effect sizes (-.20 to -.48) based on two large clinical trials. Although the FDA has not approved venlafaxine for the treatment of PTSD in the U.S., the British Association of Psychopharmacology considers venlafaxine to be a first-line medication (Baldwin et al., 2014). Venlafaxine is also one of the four antidepressants recommended by the VA/DoD (2017) and APA (2017) practice guidelines as monotherapy for PTSD in patients who choose not to engage in or are unable to access trauma-focused psychotherapy.

Other Newer Antidepressants. A number of newer antidepressants, relative to older drugs (tricyclic antidepressants and monoamine oxidase inhibitors), have been examined for their benefits in treating PTSD. These include mirtazapine, bupropion, and nefazodone. Mirtazapine (Remeron), a serotonin and norepinephrine reuptake inhibitor with antihistaminic effects, is a relatively safe antidepressant that is sedating and increases appetite in those with weight loss. Watts et al. (2013) and Lee et al. (2016) reported[1] that a single study of 29 patients (Davidson et al., 2003) found that mirtazapine's effects on PTSD symptoms did not differ from placebo over an 8-week trial on most PTSD measures. Bupropion (Wellbutrin), a norepinephrine and dopamine reuptake inhibitor (two catecholamines involved in emotional disorders), tends to increase energy, improve concentration, and reduce appetite, and like mirtazapine, is a relatively safe drug for use in middle-age and older adults with other medical problems. Based on a single trial of 22 patients (Becker et al., 2007), both Watts et al and Lee et al reported that the effect of bupropion on PTSD symptoms assessed by the Clinician Assessed PTSD Scale (CAPS; the standard measure of PTSD symptoms in clinical trials today) did not differ from placebo in the 8-week trial. Finally, nefazodone (Serzone) -- a moderate reuptake inhibitor of both serotonin and norepinephrine – is a sedating antidepressant (although less sedating than trazodone [Desyrel], its cousin). Based on a single study of 41 patients (Davis et al., 2004), nefazodone reduced PTSD symptoms on CAPS during a 12-week trial compared to placebo with a moderate ES (-.60) that achieved statistical significance (p=0.04). However, clinicians seldom use nefazodone today due to reports of liver toxicity.

Tricyclic Antidepressants (TCAs). TCAs such as amitriptyline, imipramine, nortriptyline, and desipramine are an older class of antidepressants that have lots of side-effects, including weight gain, sedation, anticholinergic, and cardiovascular effects. They are seldom used today now that SSRIs, NSRIs, and other safer antidepressants are available. Watts et al. (2013), one of the few

---

[1] Different effect sizes for this single study were reported in these two meta-analyses for reasons that are not entirely clear.

meta-analyses of TCA effectiveness in PTSD, indicated a small effect (ES=-0.36, not different from placebo) based on three studies involving 110 patients.

Monoamine Oxidase Inhibitors (MAOIs). MAOIs such a phenelzine, tranylcypromine, and brofaromine are another class of older antidepressants that block the degradation of monoamine neurotransmitters (norepinephrine, serotonin, etc.), and like TCAs, are very effective for treating depression but have a host of unpleasant side-effects (weight gain, hypotension, and hypertensive crisis unless careful with diet to avoid tyramine-containing foods/drinks). Interestingly, in the first randomized clinical trial to examine the effectiveness of medication for the treatment of PTSD in 1988, an MAOI (phenelzine) and a TCA (imipramine) were compared to placebo in 34 combat Veterans with PTSD. They found that the MAOI (compared to the TCA) was particularly more effective than placebo (Frank et al., 1988). However, Hoskins et al (2015) and Lee et al (2016), who reported on the results from two clinical trials involving the MAOI brofaromine (Consonar), did not find a difference compared to placebo when treating PTSD.

Antidepressants Overall. Watts et al (2013) reported that the overall effect of antidepressants on reducing PTSD symptoms compared to placebo in 32 randomized controlled trials involving 4,276 patients was small to moderate (ES=-.43, 95% CI=-.31 to -.53), justifying their use in the treatment of PTSD (but again as a second-line treatment after psychotherapy). Nearly three-quarters (70%) of patients with PTSD seen at VA hospitals and clinics are now prescribed an antidepressant (NPEC, 2016).

Anticonvulsants
There is uniform agreement among all the meta-analyses that anticonvulsants (i.e., anti-seizures drugs that are often used as mood stabilizers in bipolar disorder, including divalproex[Depakote], topiramate, and tiagabine, etc.) have no

role in the treatment of PTSD. In none of these reviews did the effects of anticonvulsants when used along with or combined with antidepressants exceed the effects of placebo in reducing PTSD symptoms. Watts et al. (2013) reported a meta-analysis of results from 7 studies of anticonvulsants involving 388 patients and found no significant effects compared to placebo; the same conclusion was reached by a more recent review by Lee et al (2016). There is some evidence that lamotrigine (Lamictal; an anticonvulsant used in bipolar disorder specifically for bipolar depression) has been useful in treating PTSD, although the evidence is not strong and does not justify recommending it.

Antipsychotics

Antipsychotics (used to treat psychotic symptoms), even newer second-generation drugs such as risperidone (Risperdal), olanzapine (Zyprexa), quetiapine (Seroquel), and aripiprazole (Abilify), play little role in the treatment of PTSD and none of the consensus guidelines recommend them, despite their small to moderate effects that differ significantly from placebo (ESs ranging from -.39 to -.49) (Watts et al., 2013; Lee et al., 2016). The main reason for not recommending these drugs is their side effects. Those effects include significant weight gain, increased blood sugar (especially in diabetics), risk of cardiovascular effects in older adults (including heart attack, death, and stroke), and extrapyramidal symptoms. Extrapyramidal symptoms are Parkinson-like symptoms (shaking, muscle stiffness, slowed movements) that were common in first-generation anti-psychotics like haloperidol (Haldol) or chlorpromazine (Thorazine), even though they are less common with second-generation antipsychotics. Combining antipsychotics with antidepressants does not help either, where benefits of doing so have been no greater than placebo based on a review by Lee et al (2016).

Benzodiazepines

These drugs are highly specific for relieving symptoms of anxiety and inducing sleep, and include such medications as diazepam, chlordiazepoxide, alprazolam, lorazepam, clonazepam, and sleep-enhancing agents such as temazepam and flurazepam. Most clients love these drugs since the effects that they produce are very relaxing and similar to that of alcohol intoxication. One might assume that such medications would be ideal for those with PTSD given the sedating and anxiety reducing effects of these drugs. Nevertheless, all consensus guidelines recommend against the use of benzodiazepines in treating PTSD, except in the short-term (no more than 5 days). The reason is their lack of effectiveness in reducing PTSD symptoms (Watts et al., 2013) and the potential they have for addiction. More recent reviews of pharmacological treatments for PTSD don't even mention benzodiazepines. Furthermore, benzodiazepines may interfere with memory consolidation during psychotherapy (especially with prolonged exposure), potentially worsening long-term outcomes (Otto et al., 2010; Rothbaum et al., 2014).

Other Medications

Alpha-1 adrenergic agonists such as prazosin (Minipress; a medication used to reduce blood pressure) have in recent years been praised for their effectiveness in reducing nightmares, improving sleep, and improving overall symptoms of PTSD, with relatively large effect sizes from randomized clinical trials indicating benefit (George et al., 2016). However, in the latest and most definitive randomized controlled trial examining the effects of prazosin vs. placebo on nightmares and sleep quality in 304 Veterans with PTSD, Raskind et al. (2018) reported no significant effects on any sleep parameters or PTSD symptoms, concluding that prazosin was not helpful for sleep or other distressing PTSD symptoms.

Small open trials of drugs such as N-methyl-D-aspartate (NMDA) receptor antagonists (e.g., D-cycloserine), the anxiolytic drug buspirone (Buspar), and other agents like DHEA, lithium, glucocorticoids, and cannabinoids (the active ingredient in marijuana) have shown benefit, but randomized clinical trials comparing these drugs to placebo have not yet to be done. Intravenous infusion of ketamine (Ketalar; a drug used to maintain anesthesia and an NMDA receptor antagonist), however, has been shown to cause a rapid improvement of PTSD symptoms in those with both PTSD and depressive symptoms based on one randomized clinical trial (Feder et al., 2014). More accessible methods of administering ketamine (other than IV) are now being developed such as intranasal esketamine (Ketanest), although short duration of action and side-effects remain an issue.

Beta-blockers such as propranolol (Inderal) are also being studied to reduce the hyperarousal associated with PTSD. For example, research is now being done at UCLA called "consolidation research." This is where those with PTSD are exposed to a traumatic memory and then given propranolol to block their response to the memory and consolidate the memory so it does not trigger arousal/fear (Beckers & Kindt, 2017). See below for more information on priming the brain for memory consolidation with medications.

Other Somatic Therapies

Watts et al. (2013) reported a single study of acupuncture for PTSD. In that study, Hollifield et al. (2007) compared acupuncture (1 hour twice weekly x 12 weeks) with group CBT and waitlist controls in 84 participants with PTSD. They reported a large effect for reducing PTSD (ES=-1.29, 95% CI=-.67 to -1.89; n=29), an effect that similar to that found for group CBT (-1.42; n=28), both compared to the waitlist controls (n=27). Surprisingly, dropouts were actually slightly more common in the acupuncture group compared to the other groups (34% vs. 25% and 22%, respectively). Watts et al. (2013) also reported four studies (total n=80) that examined transcranial magnetic stimulation (rTMS) for PTSD, with an effect similar to acupuncture (-1.23), although the 95% CI (+0.00 to -2.53) included 0 indicating borderline statistical significance when compared to no treatment.

Latest Medication Update

Krystal et al (2017) provide the latest treatment update and review of medications recommended for PTSD. The authors of the article were members of the PTSD Psychopharmacology Working Group that was convened in June 2016 by the VA Office of Research and Development and charged with determining the current status of drug research in PTSD and reporting on new drugs now being developed. Summarizing their recommendations, the authors stated: "The small number of informative RCTs [randomized controlled trials] in PTSD and the lack of head-to-head comparison studies contributes to the conclusion, based on meta-analysis, that pharmacotherapies are less effective than trauma-focused psychotherapies for the treatment of PTSD [citing Lee et al., 2016] and the Institute of Medicine conclusion that there is insufficient evidence on the efficacy of pharmacotherapies for the treatment of PTSD [citing IOM Report, 2007]." Krystal et al (2017) indicate that no medication other than antidepressants "meet the Phase III standards of validation" necessary to recommend them for PTSD in Veterans. However, they point out that clinicians are often desperate to prescribe something other than antidepressants. This is due to the limited effectiveness of antidepressants (the only current recommended treatment) in PTSD, the symptoms of which are often severe and poorly responsive to the best available treatments.

In addition to emphasizing the urgent need to find more effective drugs for PTSD, Krystal et al (2017) also describe novel pharmacotherapies now being examined including ketamine-like drugs, anticholinergics like scopolamine, cannabinoids with anxiolytic effects, cannabinoid receptor 1 agonists that enhance extinction (improving the effectiveness of trauma-focused psychotherapies), glucocorticoid signaling drugs, other antidepressant-like drugs such as trazodone, vortioxetine, and cyclobenzaprine, and even opioids such as buprenorphine and opioid receptor antagonists. Thus, considerable efforts are now being made to identify new medical treatments for PTSD, given the limited effectiveness of current treatments.

Medication and Psychotherapy Together

Medications can also be used in combination with psychotherapy and other psychological approaches. As in the case vignette above, antidepressants may be used to relieve intense anxiety and other symptoms of PTSD symptoms so that people feel more comfortable undergoing trauma-focused psychotherapies. In this case, medications could be prescribed prior to the initiation of psychotherapy. Other than case reports, however, there have been no randomized clinical trials examining the effectiveness of what I call "sequential treatment" (treatment with medications first, followed by psychotherapy)

The other possibility is that medications (particularly antidepressants) could be used at the same time as psychotherapy, perhaps enhancing the effectiveness of the latter. Studies of antidepressants and psychotherapy used together in order to boost effectiveness, unfortunately, have not produced very promising results, despite the strong rationale for combined treatment (VA/DoD, 2017).

Only a few studies have examined the possibility of using drugs to assist in the augmentation of trauma-focused psychotherapies, so the verdict is not yet out on these combined approaches. For example, it is known that the presence of stress hormones such as norepinephrine (noradrenaline) and hydrocortisone (cortisol) increase emotional consolidation and extinction-based types of learning (necessary for psychotherapies to be effective). In a small sample of 24 Veterans, one study found that administration of hydrocortisone at the same time as exposure to traumatic memories increased the beneficial effects of PE (Yehuda et al., 2015).

Consolidation of memory is improved by glucocorticoid (cortisol) release and beta-adrenergic receptor activity (induced by adrenaline and noradrenaline) in the basolateral nucleus of the amygdala,[1] which may decrease NMDA receptor activity. At least theoretically, then, NMDA receptor antagonists such as D-cycloserine and ketamine should facilitate habituation to trauma memories during prolonged exposure therapy. Such drugs would have to be administered immediately prior to exposure to traumatic memories that elicits distressing symptoms. While studies using D-cycloserine have not been particularly promising (Ori et al., 2015; Arman et al., 2017), there is some research in Veterans suggesting benefit (Rothbaum et al., 2014). In contrast, medications such as benzodiazepines (lorazepam, clonazepam, diazepam, etc.) may have the opposite effect, reducing stress hormones necessary for the memory consolidation and learning that are required for psychotherapy to be effective.

Conclusions

The use of medication alone for the treatment of PTSD is uniformly not recommended unless trauma-focused psychotherapies are not available, the person cannot afford them, or she or he prefers medication to psychotherapy. Antidepressants (serotonin reuptake inhibitors, in particular) are the only medications recommended by the FDA, DoD, VA, and APA. The rationale for combined treatments with both medication and psychotherapy is strong, although the results from research thus far have not been very promising. Future studies may provide further evidence supporting combined treatment. Novel medical treatments, with or without psychotherapy, are desperately needed given the relatively poor response to all available treatments at this time (Steenkamp et al., 2015; Krystal et al., 2017). This leaves the door wide open for strategies that may benefit certain subgroups of persons

---

[1]Brain region responsible for coordinating the stress-response system.

with PTSD, particularly those who are religious. That subgroup includes the majority of both U.S. Veterans and the U.S. population who report that religion is important in their lives (Koenig et al., 2018a; Gallup Poll, 2017). This leads us to our next chapter that examines religious/spiritual treatments for PTSD (and for the moral injury that often accompanies it).

Table 4.1. Medications recommended for the treatment of PTSD

Medication	Meta-analysis	No. Studies (N)	Effect Size[1]	Recommend ?
Antidepressants				
SSRIs				
Sertraline	Watts et al., 2013	7 (1,051)	-.41 (-.15 to -.66)	Yes
" "	Hoskins et al., 2015	9 (1,441)	-.13 (+.01 to -.27)	No
" "	Lee et al., 2016	7 (1,185)	-.51 -.38 to (-.64)	Yes
Paroxetine	Watts et al., 2013	6 (1,158)	-.74 (-.51 to -.97)	Yes
" "	Hoskins et al., 2015	4 (1,134)	-.43 (-.29 to -.53)	Yes
" "	Lee et al., 2016	7 (1,257)	-.36 (-.28 to -.49)	Yes
Fluoxetine	Watts et al., 2013	6 (924)	-.43 (-.25 to -.60)	Yes
" "	Hoskins et al., 2015	5 (830)	-.24 (-.08 to -.41)	Yes
" "	Lee et al., 2016	6 (1,038)	-.23 (+.39 to -.07)	No
Citalopram	Watts et al., 2013	1 (35)	+.74 (+1.45 to -.02)	No
" "	Lee et al., 2016	---	+.18 (+.91 to -.56)	No
SSRIs (overall)	Watts et al., 2013	20 (3,168)	-.48 (-.32 to -.64)	Yes
" "	Hoskins et al., 2015	21 (3,930)	-.23 (-.12 to-.33)	Yes
" "	Lee et al., 2016	---	-.37 (-.29 to -.45)	Yes
NSRIs				
Venlafaxine	Watts et al., 2013	2 (687)	-.48 (-.33 to -.63)	Yes
" "	Hoskins et al., 2015	2 (687)	-.20 (-.05 to -.35)	Yes
Newer Antidepressants				
Mirtazapine	Watts et al., 2013	1 (26) (PP)[2]	-.27 (+.52 to -1.05)	No
" "	Lee et al., 2016	1 (29) (ITT)[2]	-.81 (+.02 to -1.65)	No
Bupropion	Watts et al., 2013	1 (26)	+.21 (+.95 to -.54)	No
" "	Lee et al., 2016	1 (28)	-.22 (+.68 to -1.12)	No
Nefazodone	Davis et al. (2004)	1 (41)	-.60 (---)	No[3]
Tricyclic Antidepressants				
TCAs (overall)	Watts et al., 2013	3 (110)	-.36 (+.01 to -.74)	No
MAO Inhibitors				
Brofaromine	Hoskins et al.,2015	2 (159)	-.24 (+.33 to -.81)	No
" "	Lee et al., 2016	2 (163)	-.07 (+.22 to -.37)	No
Antidepressants (overall)	Watts et al., 2013	32 (4,276)	-.43 (-.31 to -.53)	Yes

[1] Compared to placebo control (Cohen's d or Hedges' g, where $\leq$.30=small, .50=moderate, $\geq$.80=large). When 95% confidence intervals (CI) include positive (+) numbers, the effect of the medication compared to placebo is not statistically significant. In Lee et al (2016) meta-analysis, ES is for 8-12 weeks of treatment.
[2] PP=per protocol analysis; ITT=intent to treat analysis
[3] Due to concern over liver toxicity

Table 4.1. Medications recommended for the treatment of PTSD (continued)

Medication	Meta-analysis	No. Studies (N)	Effect Size	Recommend ?
Anticonvulsants				
Divalproex	Lee et al., 2016	2 (114)	-.03 (+.41 to -.46)	No
Divalproex + antidepressant	Lee et al., 2016	---	+.38 (+1.12 to -.36)	No
Topiramate	Hoskins et al., 2015	2 (69)	-.46 (+.02 to -.94)	No
" "	Lee et al., 2016	2 (75)	-.34 (+.14 to -.82)	No
Tiagabine	Lee et al., 2016	2 (258)	+.02 (+.28 to -.24)	No
Anticonvulsants (overall)	Watts et al., 2013	7 (388)	-.23 (+.14 to -.59)	No
" "	Lee et al., 2016	---	-.03 (+.17 to -.22)	No
Antipsychotics				
Risperidone	Watts et al., 2013	7 (450)	-.41 (-.12 to -.70)	(?)
" "	Lee et al., 2016	5 (422)	-.48 (+.14 to -1.10)	No
Risperidone + antidepressant	Lee et al., 2016	---	-.19 (+.64 to -.98)	No
Olanzapine	Watts et al., 2013	2 (34)	+.10 (+1.52 to -1.31)	No
" "	Hoskins et al., 2015	2 (39)	-.61 (+.05 to -1.27)	No
" "	Lee et al., 2016	3 (64)	-.72 (-.09 to -1.36)	(?)
Olanzapine + antidepressant	Lee et al., 2016	---	-.80 (+.14 to -1.73)	No
Aripiprazole+antidepressant	Lee et al., 2016	1 (16)	-.03 (+1.02 to -1.08)	No
Antipsychotics (overall)	Watts et al., 2013	9 (484)	-.39 (-.05 to -.66)	No
" "	Lee et al., 2016	---	-.49 (-.15 to -.83)	(?)
Benzodiazepines (overall)	Watts et al., 2013	1 (10)	-.28 (+.87 to -1.43)	No
Other Medications				
Prazosin (α-1 adrenergic)	Watts et al., 2013	2 (54)	-.78 (+1.82 to -.27)	No
" "	George et al., 2016	6 (191)		
	- nightmares		-1.02 (-.41 to -1.62)	Yes
	- sleep quality		-.93 (+.02 to -1.88)	No
	- sleep quality		-1.14 (-.24 to -2.03)	Yes
	- illness severity		-1.20 (-.79 to -1.61)	Yes
NMDA or D-cycloserine) (glutamatergic)	Watts et al., 2013	2 (28)	-.24 (+.94 to -.46)	No
Medications (overall)	Lee et al., 2016	---	-.43 (-.36 to -.49)	Yes
Other Somatic Treatments				
Acupuncture	Watts et al., 2013	1 (84)	-1.29 (-.67 to -1.89)	(?)
Transcranial Magnetic Stimulation (rTMS)	Watts et al., 2013	4 (80)	-1.23 (+0.00 to -2.53)	(?)

5 THE ROLE OF RELIGIOUS FAITH

Psychological and medical treatments for PTSD, while effective and helpful for many people who struggle with this disorder, are often not enough. Something more is needed for the complete healing of those with PTSD. Religious or spiritual (R/S) approaches may help to fill this void. I examine here a range of R/S treatments for PTSD, as well as those for moral injury, which as noted in Chapter 2 often accompanies PTSD and may interfere with recovery. At the present time, there are few evidence-based R/S treatments for PTSD or moral injury (MI). Nevertheless, all five major world religions have been dealing with both PTSD and MI for thousands of years, so there is a lot to learn from these time-tested approaches that have for generations proven effective. The evidence for their effectiveness, however, is not randomized clinical trials, but rather the stories recorded in the sacred scriptures and the testimonials of many who have suffered from PTSD and overcome it through their faith. As in Chapter 3 on psychotherapies for PTSD, this discussion will be divided into trauma-focused and non-trauma-focused therapies, and further subdivided into treatments provided by licensed mental health professionals and treatments provided by chaplains or other clergy (see Koenig et al., 2019 for a more detailed description of S/R treatments).

Trauma-Focused R/S Therapies

Trauma-focused R/S therapies that are usually administered by licensed mental health professionals include Building Spiritual Strengths (BSS) and Spiritually Integrated Cognitive Processing Therapy (SICPT). In addition, there are Mindfulness-based Stress Reduction (MBSR) therapies grounded in the Buddhist religious tradition and Mantram-based therapies grounded in the Hindu faith tradition. I will describe each of these briefly below.

<u>Building Spiritual Strengths</u>. BSS is a manual-based group therapy intervention that is administered by either mental health professionals or religious professionals with additional mental health training (master's degrees in some type of counseling, either pastoral counseling, marital and family therapy, or other degrees resulting in professional licensure). BSS is an interfaith intervention for both military personnel and civilians (manuals exist to guide therapy in each). BSS is delivered during two-hour weekly group therapy sessions over eight weeks. This intervention focuses on both PTSD and the religious aspects of moral injury that accompany it. Pre-existing faith resources of individuals are utilized to address trauma-related spiritual concerns in an attempt to resolve spiritual struggles that are impeding the use of spiritual resources to cope with the trauma. Groups may be held either at the VA hospital or in religious community settings.

Two randomized clinical trials have now demonstrated the effectiveness of BSS group therapy in reducing PTSD symptoms in Veterans with significant trauma (Harris et al., 2011; Harris et al., 2018). In the first study of 54 Veterans, compared to a waitlist control arm, the effect size (ES) of BSS on reducing PTSD symptoms was -0.72, indicating a medium to large effect (Harris et al., 2011). In the second study of 138 Veterans, Harris et al. (2018) compared BSS to another active treatment, Present Center Group Therapy (PCT). While no difference in PTSD symptoms was found between treatment groups by the end of treatment, both BSS and PCT significantly reduced PTSD symptoms; the ES for BSS was -1.06 and for PCT was -0.92, both indicating large clinically meaningful symptom reductions. Long term follow-up beyond the last evaluation of treatment effects 2-months after the end of treatment, however, was not conducted. While there was no difference between BSS and PCT in lowering PTSD symptoms, BSS was more effective than PCT in reducing Divine Struggles (i.e., struggles in the person's relationship with God).

Spiritually Integrated Cognitive Processing Therapy (SICPT). SICPT is a recently developed manual-based psychotherapy that targets moral injury in the setting of PTSD. SICPT integrates spirituality into standard CPT-C, with a special focus on MI (Koenig et al., 2017; Pearce et al., 2018). SICPT is primarily for those who indicate that religion is important or very important in their lives. SICPT targets dysfunctional trauma-related beliefs and assumptions (called "stuck points") and the accompanying inner moral and ethical conflicts. Scriptures are used to challenge dysfunctional cognitions; clients are encouraged to re-engage in their faith community; religious rituals are utilized to facilitate forgiveness; and emphasis is placed on atonement. As noted earlier, we think that reducing MI will decrease PTSD symptoms as well, enabling those with PTSD to utilize their religious resources more fully in dealing with the trauma and respond more readily to secular treatments as well. We also think that addressing MI will reduce some of the mental and social problems that often accompany PTSD, including depressive, anxiety, substance use disorders, and family problems. Religion-specific versions of SICPT have also been developed for use in Christian, Jewish, Muslim, Hindu, and Buddhist clients (Pearce et al., 2017).

Although the effectiveness of SICPT has not yet been examined in a randomized clinical trial, pilot work shows that this treatment is effective for reducing both moral injury and PTSD symptoms (O'Garo & Koenig, 2018, unpublished data). A randomized clinical trial will soon be conducted in Veterans with PTSD symptoms and moral injury at the Greater Los

Angeles Veterans Affairs Health System (VA Research Currents, 2018).

Mindfulness-based Stress Reduction (MBSR). MBSR is a Buddhist-grounded intervention based on the seventh step of the Eightfold Path of Buddhism. Mindfulness involves maintaining a focus on the present moment, putting away all worldly desires, and becoming aware of emotions and feelings as simply what they are, without attachment to them. MBSR therapies are typically administered in eight 2.5-hour group sessions over eight weeks (although can also be administered as a one-on-one individual sessions). Many therapists think that this is a secular intervention (or has been secularized), but it is not. One could just as well do Centering Prayer with Christian clients to achieve these goals, but this is typically not offered. Instead, MBSR is administered to everyone regardless of religious affiliation. So much for patient-centered care.

Nevertheless, there is considerable research examining the effectiveness of MBSR therapies in the treatment of PTSD. In a meta-analysis of 18 randomized clinical trials, Hopwood and Schutte (2017) reported that the average effect size was -0.44 (95% CI=-0.61 to -0.27). Thus, MBSR therapies have a small to moderate effect in reducing PTSD symptoms. The treatment is generally less effective than other trauma-focused therapies. However, for Buddhists with PTSD, it may be an excellent therapy.

Mantram Repetition Therapy (MRT). In MRT, the person with PTSD learns to silently repeat a mantra (sacred word), which enables her or him to slow their thoughts and bring those thoughts to a single point of attention. Just as MBSR is a Buddhist form of treatment, MRT is solidly based within Hindu philosophy and practice (i.e., is a Hindu form of meditation). The treatment is administered in eight 60-minute individual one-on-one sessions over eight weeks. Studies on the effectiveness of MRT have primarily been done by a single research group, Jill Bormann and colleagues at San Diego State University. In all three of these studies, MRT has been effective in reducing PTSD symptoms in Veterans. In the latest study of 173 Veterans, published in the *American Journal of Psychiatry*, Bormann et al (2018) reported that MRT was moderately more effective than Patient Centered Therapy in reducing PTSD symptoms (ES=-0.49 by the end of treatment). However, as in secular psychotherapies described in Chapter 3, the majority of participants continued to have significant PTSD symptoms after treatment.

<u>Other Trauma-Focused R/S Therapies</u>. Several other trauma-based therapies either have a R/S component or focus entirely on R/S. These include Impact of Killing (IOK) in war therapy, Spiritual Hypnosis Assisted Therapy (SHAT), and trauma-focused pastoral counseling, and trauma-focused religious counseling. IOK therapy addresses both symptoms of PTSD and the moral struggles that military personnel may experience as a result of killing in combat. This includes exploring spiritual concerns with regard to killing and reconnecting to a spiritual community. In a pilot study of Veterans, Maguen and colleagues (2017) found that the IOK intervention significantly reduced PTSD symptoms, depression, and anxiety compared to a group receiving no treatment. SHAT is a Hindu-based therapy where clients meditate while breathing deeply through the nose and exhaling through the mouth, and once a trance is induced, therapists guide participants to reframe the meaning of traumatic memories in spiritual terms. Some benefit from this treatment has been documented in Hindu children recovering from a natural disaster (Lesmana et al., 2009).

Trauma-focused pastoral counseling and religious counseling are provided by licensed professional counselors who specifically uses a person's religious beliefs, along with psychological counsel, to help him or her heal from PTSD. To my knowledge, there have been no randomized clinical trials examining the efficacy of pastoral counseling for PTSD, although there have been case reports describing its benefits (Rogers & Koenig, 2013). Religious counseling is similar to pastoral counseling and delivered by licensed professional counselors. A specific religion is usually utilized in treatment depending on the clients' faith tradition. For example, there are Christian counselors, Jewish counselors, and Muslim counselors who only treat patients from these religious traditions. For example, Christian counselors often use the Bible to guide clients in altering their dysfunctional cognitions related to trauma and changing behavior, although supplement this with various traditional counseling techniques. To my knowledge, again only case reports and personal testimonials exist for the effectiveness of religious counseling for PTSD (Gingrich, 2013).

Non-Trauma-Focused Therapies
These are religious or spiritual psychotherapies that do not focus on the traumatic event, but address PTSD symptoms more generally. While these non-trauma-focused R/S therapies may be useful in the treatment of PTSD, no studies have yet examined their effectiveness in this disorder. I now review religious cognitive behavioral therapy (RCBT) and other spiritually-integrated therapies.

    <u>Religious Cognitive Behavioral Therapy (RCBT)</u>. Given that cognitive processing therapy (CPT) is a variant of cognitive behavioral therapy (CBT), it is not a great jump to imagine that religiously-integrated CBT might also help to relieve symptoms of PTSD. Furthermore, "trauma-focused" CBT has been shown to be effective in the treatment of PTSD (with an average ES of -1.37; Lee et al., 2016), providing further rationale for RCBT. RCBT is a manual-based structured intervention for the treatment of depression. It has been examined in a randomized clinical trial in persons with chronic medical illness and found to reduce depressive symptoms on the Beck Depression Inventory to a similar degree as achieved by conventional CBT (CCBT), with a large effect size (within-group ES=-3.02 for RCBT compared to ES=-2.39 for CCBT; between group difference ES=0.12) (Koenig et al., 2015; Koenig, 2018b). However, RCBT was significantly more effective than CCBT among those

who were more religious at the start of therapy (group by religiosity interaction was significant at p<0.05). Thus, RCBT may be recommended for those with depression and chronic medical illness who are particularly religious.

RCBT may also be helpful for the negative cognitions and mood symptom cluster (Criterion D) in those with PTSD, even if the treatment does not specifically focus on the traumatic event. Improving negative mood and cognitions may help with the other symptoms of PTSD and other problems such as depressive and anxiety disorders that often accompany PTSD. These musing are only hypothetical, however, since no randomized clinical trial examining RCBT has been conducted in PTSD. Note that Christian, Jewish, Muslim, Hindu, and Buddhist versions of RCBT have been developed and treatment manuals are available free on our website (CSTH, 2014).

<u>Other Spiritually-Integrated Non-Trauma-Focused Therapies</u>. There are a number of spiritually integrated psychotherapies developed for treating individuals with other emotional disorders, although not specifically for those with PTSD. Psychologist Ken Pargament has described many of these interventions (see Pargament, 2011).

Pastoral Care and Support

Clergy and chaplains, although not usually licensed professional counselors, nevertheless provide an enormous amount of pastoral care and support. Pastoral care and support does not require state licensure and, in fact, is probably more commonly sought by persons with PTSD and their families than all of the above treatments combined (including more common than trauma-focused psychotherapies described in Chapter 3). Many individuals with emotional and family problems consult clergy first when having difficulty. Because of their sheer number (over 350,000 in the U.S. alone), clergy provide nearly as much counseling as the entire membership of the American Psychological Association (Weaver, 1995). Furthermore, clergy are as likely to see those with serious mental disorders as are mental health professionals (Larson et al., 1988). Unfortunately, there are no randomized clinical trials examining the effectiveness of pastoral care and support in the treatment of PTSD. This is likely the result of lack of government funding for clinical trials in this area, although that does not negate the effectiveness of such approaches.

A similar situation is present for chaplains. While board-certified chaplains require training in clinical pastoral education (CPE), complete an internship in a clinical setting, and need to obtain continuing education credits each year to maintaining their board certification, they are not licensed by the state or considered professional counselors. However, chaplains do a lot of informal counseling for people with PTSD and their families, especially for Veterans and active duty military personnel. Again, there is almost no research on the effectiveness of chaplain interventions in PTSD, although studies demonstrate their effectiveness of chaplain visits in medical settings. We have developed a series of chaplain interventions for moral injury in the setting of PTSD and are planning to test the effectiveness of these religion-specific chaplain interventions (Christian, Jewish, Muslim, Hindu, Buddhist) for MI and PTSD in the randomized clinical trial (Ames et al., 2018). As noted earlier, the sacred scriptures from all major faith traditions address issues pertaining to MI, trauma, and loss, and have done so for thousands of years (Koenig et al., 2019).

Other Religious/Spiritual Treatments. Several other religious/spiritual treatments may be helpful for PTSD, including both trauma-focused and non-trauma-focused interventions. Among the trauma-focused therapies proposed for PTSD are Shamanic treatment (Whabeh et al., 2017; case series only) and religious writing about trauma (Chen, 2005). The latter is a novel and simple intervention that involves writing about the traumatic event from a religious perspective. This is a variant of written exposure therapy (discussed in Chapter 3) that has now been compared to non-religious narrative writing in two randomized clinical trials and found to have superior results in reducing symptoms of PTSD and depression, particularly in those with more severe trauma symptoms (Chen, 2005; Chen & Contrada, 2009).

Non-trauma focused interventions shown to be effective in randomized clinical trials tend to be religion-specific. For Christians, a prayer intervention has been shown to be more effective in reducing depression than standard care in a clinical trial conducted among medical patients seen in primary care (Boelens et al., 2012). For Muslims, Muslim prayer (Delghani et al., 2012) and reciting the Qur'an (Babamohammadi et al., 2015) for the treatment of anxiety (which is a major aspect of PTSD) have both been shown to be more effective than comparison groups in medical settings.

Moral Injury

MI, as noted earlier, is common among those with PTSD. Many of the R/S treatments directed at PTSD may also be helpful for MI, and sometimes address it specifically as a separate problem. Interventions used to treat moral injury in clients with co-existing PTSD symptoms include Building Spiritual Strengths (BSS) group therapy and Impact of Killing (IOK) in war, and Spiritually Integrated Cognitive Processing Therapy (SICPT), all discussed earlier. Only SICPT, however, was developed specifically to treat MI in those with PTSD. As noted earlier, we have developed five religion-specific appendices for SICPT for licensed professional therapists and five religion-specific versions for chaplains that specifically target the 10 major symptoms of moral injury (Pearce et al., 2017; Ames et al., 2018). If you or a family member has PTSD and are exhibiting some of the symptoms of moral injury (see **Table 6.1**, next chapter), I encourage you to find someone who would be willing to try one of these therapies. As I've indicated many times in this book, reducing moral injury is likely to have a significant impact on reducing PTSD symptoms and the psychiatric, social, and behavioral problems that often accompany PTSD.

Conclusions

A number of religious/spiritual interventions have been developed specifically for the treatment of PTSD or for the moral injury that frequently accompanies it. I have reviewed those treatments above, categorizing them into trauma-focused and non-trauma-focused therapies. Among trauma-focused interventions delivered by licensed mental health professionals are Building Spiritual Strengths, Spiritually Integrated Cognitive Processing Therapy, Buddhist Mindfulness-based Stress Reduction therapies, Hindu Mantram Repetition Therapy, and Impact of Killing in War Therapy. Non-trauma-focused interventions include Religious Cognitive Behavioral Therapy, other Spiritually-Integrated Therapies, Pastoral Counseling, and Religious Counseling. There are also many trauma-focused and non-focused therapies that can be administered by clergy and chaplains who are not licensed by the state to provide formal counseling nor are specific trained in mental health. However, these religious professionals probably see more people with PTSD and moral injury than do licensed mental health professionals. The reason for this is that seeing clergy and chaplains for emotional problems carries with it no stigma and has no cost (clergy and chaplains do not ordinarily charge for their services). Some of the psychotherapeutic interventions described for licensed mental health professionals in this chapter have been examined in randomized clinical trials and found to be as effective if not more so than secular therapies, particularly in those who are religious. Religious/spiritual interventions may fill an important gap in the treatment of PTSD, and especially for those with accompanying moral injury.

6 SUMMARY & RECOMMENDATIONS

In this short volume I have described what PTSD is, the causes and protective factors, associated psychiatric and moral syndromes, and psychological, medical, and religious/spiritual treatments for this disorder and the moral injury that often accompanies it. I will briefly summarize the major points made here and then go on to make recommendations for individuals who struggle with this disorder and members of their family.

Summary of Points

1. Posttraumatic stress disorder is a diagnosable mental health problem with specific symptoms that are disabling and destroy quality of life for the person and their family. This disorder emerges after a severe traumatic stressor that threatens the life or physical integrity of a person or loved ones. There are factors that increase vulnerability to PTSD and also certain characteristics that make people more resistant to PTSD following severe stress. PTSD is also often accompanied by other psychiatric problems that were present either before PTSD (increasing vulnerability to it) or arose after PTSD as a consequence of distressing symptoms (i.e., intrusive flashbacks and nightmares, avoidance behaviors, negative emotions and thoughts about self and others, increased irritability and hypervigilance). These problems include depressive disorder,

anxiety disorder, substance use disorders, and disruption of relationships with family and friends.

2. Moral injury often accompanies PTSD and is reflected by inner conflict manifested by both psychological and religious/spiritual symptoms. Psychological symptoms include guilt, shame, feelings of betrayal by others, moral concerns over having transgressed moral values, loss of meaning and purpose in life, loss of trust in others, difficulty forgiving, and self-condemnation. Religious/spiritual symptoms include religious struggles (anger at God, feeling punished by God, difficulty forgiving God, deserted by one's religious community, etc.) and experiencing a loss or weakening of religious faith. Moral injury is associated with more severe PTSD symptoms, depression, anxiety, and suicidal thoughts and behaviors. Moral injury, then, is a serious syndrome with multiple psychiatric and social consequences and is of special concern because it may block the successful treatment of PTSD.

3. A number of secular psychological treatments have been developed and tested for the treatment of PTSD. The two evidence-based psychotherapies for PTSD that are recommended by the Veterans Affairs, the Department of Defense, and the American Psychological Association are Prolonged Exposure (PE) and Cognitive Processing Therapy (CPT). Both of these treatments have been shown in randomized clinical trials to have large clinically meaningful effects when compared to no treatment, although often leave clients with residual PTSD symptoms and only in a minority of cases result in a complete remission of the disorder. Even these positive results have been obtained in clinical trials that include only the healthiest of individuals, those without suicidal ideation or other serious psychiatric disorders (who are usually excluded from clinical trials or do not volunteer to participate in such research). There are also a number of trauma-focused and non-trauma focused therapies whose effectiveness has been

examined in scientific studies; however, they do not appear to be as effective as PE or CPT. Many of the secular therapies for PTSD also claim to address moral injury, although the latter is seldom a focus of treatment or measured as an outcome.

4. Medications are often used to treat PTSD. However, current treatment guidelines indicate that medication should only be used to treat PTSD if trauma-focused therapies are not available or if the person cannot afford the therapy or prefers medication. The only medications currently recommended for PTSD are antidepressants, specifically serotonin reuptake inhibitors or norepinephrine-serotonin reuptake inhibitors. Many other medications and somatic therapies, however, have been tried in the treatment of PTSD, largely because of the poor results that antidepressants usually produce. I have comprehensively reviewed those medications and examined their effects when compared to placebo in clinical trials. Combination of psychotherapy and medication has also been discussed, as has the possibility that certain drugs may prime the brain to be more responsive to PE or CPT, although the results of clinical trials on treatment combinations have been disappointing.

5. Given that current treatments for PTSD often leave people with residual symptoms and seldom result in complete remission, there is plenty of room for improvement in the treatment of this disabling disorder. As a result, the door is wide open for novel treatments including religious/spiritual approaches that hold promise for a more complete healing from PTSD than secular therapies alone can achieve, particularly among individuals who say that religion is important to them. Religious/spiritual beliefs and practices represent key resources that may help to either prevent the onset of PTSD or speed recovery, as numerous research studies have shown. Consequently, a number of religious/spiritual interventions have been developed and tested in randomized clinical trials for

their effectiveness in relieving the symptoms of PTSD and the moral injury that often accompanies it. The two interventions that have the greatest potential in this regard are Building Spiritual Strengths group therapy and one-on-one Spiritually Integrated Cognitive Processing Therapy that target both PTSD and moral injury. There are also Eastern spiritual interventions including Buddhist mindfulness-based therapies and Hindu mantram repetition that have been shown to improve PTSD symptoms. Finally, there are many religious interventions based on the holy scriptures of the five major religious traditions that have for millennia addressed the problems of trauma from war and severe loss through religious beliefs, rituals and practices. Clergy and chaplains both historically and today continue to help many of those suffering from PTSD, although they are often not acknowledged by mental health professionals because the work that they do has seldom been subject to the gold standard randomized clinical trial. Nevertheless, the wisdom gained from religious scriptures and faith traditions can make a real difference in the treatment of PTSD, perhaps producing results that are more complete and permanent.

Recommendations for Individuals with PTSD

1. If you (or a family member) have PTSD symptoms like those described in Chapter 1 and are suffering and distressed by these symptoms and willing to do whatever it takes to feel better, congratulations. Yes, congratulations, because you are at an important transition point in your life. Perhaps at no other time than this one will real transformation be as possible for you. It is only during times of pain and suffering that people are willing to change. In fact, the brain and central nervous system are known to be more plastic or malleable at times of high stress (McEwen & Gianaros, 2011). With some guidance and wise advice and considerable effort on your part, it is now possible for your life to become more meaningful, more fulfilling, and more capable of making positive difference in others' lives in ways that you may have never thoughts possible (and could not

happen if you had not experienced the trauma that is causing your distress now). As crazy as this may seem, your traumatic experience could actually be a blessing in your life. But only you can make this a reality by taking advantage of your situation, seeing it as an *opportunity* for growth and transformation, and committing to the effort necessary for this transformation to occur.

2. The second step is to seek help and guidance. First, you need to see a mental health professional who can make the diagnosis of PTSD or determine if there is some other psychiatric or emotional problem that is present. Effective treatment will differ depend on the particular condition that is present (just like any medical illness where treatments will vary depending on the particular diagnosis).

3. Consider obtaining psychotherapy from a mental health professional who is experienced in treating individuals with PTSD using one of the two recommended treatment approaches: Prolonged Exposure (PE) Therapy or Cognitive Processing Therapy (CPT-C).

4. Be willing to take medication prescribed by a PTSD expert if recommended by your therapist. However, don't think that medications are a quick fix or will solve all of your problems. They won't. Research shows that hard work in psychotherapy has the greatest effect on reducing PTSD symptoms, providing nearly double the benefit that medication alone produces.

5. If religion is important to you, find out from your therapist whether he or she would be willing to utilize your religious beliefs/practices as a resource in the treatment, or if the therapist knows of a chaplain or clergy person who is experienced at dealing with individuals suffering from severe trauma and can assist you with any religious struggles or symptoms of moral injury that you may be having. If you are in

the military and on active duty, remember that unlike behavioral health specialists, chaplains are not required to reveal anything about your mental condition to your commander.

6. At the same time that you are seeking professional help from a licensed mental health professional and a clergyperson or chaplain, there are things that you can do on your own to help yourself, especially if you are religious (even if you are not religious but realize the wisdom contained in the ancient scriptures). Here are a few scriptures that you can meditate on, depending on your faith tradition:

Christians

But God demonstrates his own love for us in this: While we were still sinners, Christ died for us. (Romans 5:8)[4]

Who shall separate us from the love of Christ? Shall trouble or hardship or persecution or famine or nakedness or danger or sword? As it is written:
"For your sake we face death all day long; we are considered as sheep to be slaughtered."
No, in all these things we are more than conquerors through him who loved us. For I am convinced that neither death nor life, neither angels nor demons, neither the present nor the future, nor any powers, neither height nor depth, nor anything else in all creation, will be able to separate us from the love of God that is in Christ Jesus our Lord. (Romans 8:35-39)

Even though I was once a blasphemer and a persecutor and a violent man, I was shown mercy because I acted in ignorance and unbelief. The grace of our Lord was poured out on me abundantly, along with the faith and love that are in Christ Jesus.
Here is a trustworthy saying that deserves full acceptance:

---

[4] New International Version of the Holy Bible

Christ Jesus came into the world to save sinners—of whom I am the worst. (1 Timothy 1:13-15)

Jews

Worship the L-RD your G-d, and his blessing will be on your food and water. I will take away sickness from among you (Exodus 23:25)

And he passed in front of Moses, proclaiming, "The L-RD, the L-RD, the compassionate and gracious G-d, slow to anger, abounding in love and faithfulness, maintaining love to thousands, and forgiving wickedness, rebellion and sin. (Exodus 34:6-7)

I say this because I know what I am planning for you," says the L-RD. "I have good plans for you, not plans to hurt you. I will give you hope and a good future. Then you will call my name. You will come to me and pray to me, and I will listen to you. You will search for me. And when you search for me with all your heart, you will find me! (Jeremiah 29:11-13)

So do not fear, for I am with you; do not be dismayed, for I am your G-d.
I will strengthen you and help you; I will uphold you with my righteous right hand. (Isaiah 41:10)

Muslims

When you have decided on a course of action, put your trust in God: God loves those who put their trust in Him. (Qur'an 3: 159)[5]

Truly it is the remembrance of God that hearts find peace. (Qur'an 13:28)

---

[5] The Qur'an: A new translation by M.A.S. Abdel Haleem (Oxford World's Classics, 2004)

Your Lord says, "Call on Me and I will answer you..." (Qur'an 40:60)

God will be enough for those who put their trust in Him…after hardship, God will bring ease. (Qur'an 65:3,7)

Hindus

You are qualified simply with regard to action, never with regard to its results. You must be neither motivated by the results of action nor attached to inaction. (Bhagavad Gita 2:47)[6]

The wise call him a man of learning whose every activity is free from desire and specific intention; his actions are consumed in the fire of knowledge. That man who depends upon nothing, who has given up attachment to the results of action, is perpetually satisfied… (Bhagavad Gita 4:19-20)

Even if you are the very worst of all transgressors, with the boat of knowledge you shall plot a safe course through all crookedness. (Bhagavad Gita 4:36)

Fix your mind on me [Lord Krishnan, i.e., the Supreme God], devote yourself to me, sacrifice me, do homage to me, and so you shall in reality come to me. I promise you: you are dear to me. Abandoning all duties, vow yourself to me alone. Don't agonize, I shall release you from all evils. (Bhagavad-Gita 18:65-66)

Buddhists

By faith, by virtue and energy, by deep contemplation and vision, by wisdom and by right action, you shall overcome the sorrows of life. (Dhammapada 144)

---

[6] The Bhagavad Gita: A new translation by W.J. Johnson (Oxford World's Classics, 1994)

Misery, the arising of misery, and the transcending of misery, the Noble Eightfold Path leading to the allaying of misery. (Dhammapada 191)[7]

Ah, so pleasantly we live without enmity among those with enmity. Among humans with enmity do we dwell without enmity. (Dhammapada 197)

Those who see what is not fear as fear, and see no fear in fear, ones who endorse wrong views, such beings go to a state of woe…. But having known error as error, and non-error as non-error, ones who endorse proper views, such beings go to a state of weal [a healthy, prosperous life]. (Dhammapada 317, 319)

7. Get a copy of the book "You are My Beloved. Really?" (Koenig, 2016) and read it. Not just once but go through it repeatedly until you begin feeling like you are truly His beloved.

Recommendations for Family Members

1. If you think that a family member might be suffering from PTSD, then encourage her or him to get help. If your loved one refuses to see a mental health professional, then encourage them to see their medical doctor, a chaplain or a clergy person. Be sure that person has experience treating people with PTSD (if he or she is a Veteran, they should seek help at a local VA).

2. What can you do to help? Don't put pressure on your loved one to talk. However, be present so that when they feel ready to talk, you are there. When they are ready to talk, listen. Listen, listen, listen. Don't offer advice or try to solve their problem. And don't say that you understand what they are going through. Instead, have them teach you what they are having to endure.

---

[7] The Dhammapada: The Sayings of the Buddha (Oxford World's Classics, 2000)

3. If your loved one is acting out and behaving in destructive ways to themselves, to you, or to others, set limits on their behavior. In a kind but firm manner, indicate what the limits are and stick to those limits no matter what, even if it hurts (and it will hurt). However, the pain will be a lot less now than it will be in the long run if you don't stick to your limits. One consequence of transgressing those limits may be that you have to temporarily move out of the house.

4. Get help for yourself. If you are religious person, then pour all your effort into developing your spiritual life. This will be your greatest asset as you face the storm of PTSD in your partner.

5. If you are not already involved in a faith community, do so. If you are involved in a faith community and you are not actively engaged in it, then start. Identify (carefully) a group of people in your faith community who are willing to support you. Your clergy person may help you identify such a person/s, if you cannot find them on your own. If your loved one with PTSD is willing, encourage them to go with you. However, do not bug them about it; just offer and then let it rest. Also, do not spend so much time engaged in religious community activities or with your support people that you neglect your family member at home, even if it is difficult to be around them.

6. If your loved one obtained a copy of "You are My Beloved. Really?" then read it, either on your own alone or with your loved one. As suggested above, don't read it just once, but read it over and over again until you feel like His beloved. Also, see the holy scriptures above to meditate on, depending on your faith tradition.

Conclusion

The reader of this little book now knows a lot more about PTSD and its treatments than he or she did before. Although PTSD is a terrible and destructive disorder that wreaks havoc in the lives of many people and their families, there are treatments now available that can help. While secular trauma-focused psychotherapies and medication can help enormously, they are seldom enough. The major religious traditions in the world have for millennia dealt with trauma, loss, suffering, and pain, so take advantage of this ancient wisdom. Religious/spiritual resources and treatment approaches may help to fill the gap that traditional therapies often cannot, so don't underestimate the power of faith in the achieving complete healing from PTSD and the moral struggles that often accompany this disorder.

Table 6.1. Moral Injury Symptoms Scale – Military Version – Short Form (MISS-M-SF)©

Instructions: Please circle <u>the number</u> that most accurately indicates how you are feeling now:

1. I feel betrayed by leaders who I once trusted.

1	2	3	4	5	6	7	8	9	10
Strongly disagree		Mildly disagree		Neutral		Mildly agree			Strongly agree

2. I feel guilt over failing to save the life of someone in war.

1	2	3	4	5	6	7	8	9	10
Strongly disagree		Mildly disagree		Neutral		Mildly agree			Strongly agree

3. I feel ashamed about what I did or did not do during this time.

1	2	3	4	5	6	7	8	9	10
Strongly disagree		Mildly disagree		Neutral		Mildly agree			Strongly agree

4. I am troubled by having acted in ways that violated my own morals or values.

1	2	3	4	5	6	7	8	9	10
Strongly disagree		Mildly disagree		Neutral		Mildly agree			Strongly agree

5. Most people are trustworthy.

1	2	3	4	5	6	7	8	9	10
Strongly disagree		Disagree		Neutral		Agree			Strongly agree

6. I have a good sense of what makes my life meaningful.

1	2	3	4	5	6	7	8	9	10
Absolutely untrue	Mostly untrue	Somewhat untrue	Can't say true or false	Somewhat true	Mostly true				Absolutely true

7. I have forgiven myself for what happened to me or others during combat.

1	2	3	4	5	6	7	8	9	10
Strongly disagree		Disagree		Neutral		Agree			Strongly agree

8. All in all, I am inclined to feel that I am a failure.

1	2	3	4	5	6	7	8	9	10
Strongly disagree		Disagree		Neutral		Agree			Strongly agree

9. I wondered what I did for God to punish me.

1	2	3	4	5	6	7	8	9	10
A great deal (very true)		Quite a bit			Somewhat				Not at all (very untrue)

10. *Compared to when you first went into the military* has your religious faith since then...

1	2	3	4	5	6	7	8	9	10
Weakened a lot		Weakened a little			Strengthened a little				Strengthened a lot

Do the feelings you indicated above cause you significant distress or impair your ability to function in relationships, at work, or other areas of life important to you? (check one of the following):[1]

☐ Not at All   ☐ Mild   ☐ Moderate   ☐ Very Much   ☐ Extremely

---

[1] In other words, "If you indicated <u>any</u> problems above, how <u>difficult</u> have these problems made it for you to do your work, take care of things at home, or get along with other people?"

Scoring: Reverse score items 5, 6, 7, 9, and 10, and then sum all items to produce a total score indicating moral injury severity (possible range 10-100)

Source: Koenig et al (2018b)

REFERENCES

American Psychiatric Association. (2013). *Diagnostic and Statistical Manual of Mental Disorders (DSM-5®)*. Washington, DC: American Psychiatric Publishing

Ames D, Haynes K, Adamson SF, Bruce LE, Chacko BK, Button L, Fleming W, Luoma J, Price RA, Kopacz MS, Oliver JP, Daza SI, Koenig HG (2018). A structured chaplain intervention for Veterans with moral injury in the setting of PTSD (*Christian Version*). Durham, NC: Duke University Center for Spirituality, Theology and Health (Buddhist, Hindu, Jewish, and Muslim versions also available; contact Harold.Koenig@duke.edu)

APA (2017). American Psychological Association Guideline for the Treatment of Posttraumatic Stress Disorder in Adults (adopted as APA Policy on February 24, 2017). Retrieved on 6/24/18 from http://www.apa.org/ptsd-guideline/.

Arman, S., Soheilimehr, A., & Maracy, M. R. (2017). The efficacy of augment of D-cycloserine and cognitive behavioral therapy on adolescent with one type of anxiety disorders: A double-blind randomized controlled trial. *Advanced Biomedical Research* 6:11.

Babamohammadi H, Sotodehasl N, Koenig HG, Jahani C, Ghorbani R (2015). The effect of Qur'an recitation on anxiety in hemodialysis patients: A randomized clinical trial. *Journal of Religion and Health* 54(5):1921-1930

Baldwin, D. S. et al. (2014). Evidence-based pharmacological treatment of anxiety disorders, post-traumatic stress disorder and obsessive-compulsive disorder: a revision of the 2005 guidelines from the British Association for Psychopharmacology. *Journal of Psychopharmacology*, *28*(5), 403-439.

Becker, M. E., Hertzberg, M. A., Moore, S. D., Dennis, M. F., Bukenya, D. S., & Beckham, J. C. (2007). A placebo-controlled trial of bupropion SR in the treatment of chronic posttraumatic stress disorder. *Journal of Clinical Psychopharmacology, 27*(2), 193-197.

Beckers, T., & Kindt, M. (2017). Memory reconsolidation interference as an emerging treatment for emotional disorders: strengths, limitations, challenges, and opportunities. *Annual Review of Clinical Psychology* 13:99-121.

Bernardy, N. C., Lund, B. C., Alexander, B., & Friedman, M. J. (2012). Prescribing trends in veterans with posttraumatic stress disorder. *Journal of Clinical Psychiatry 73*(3), 297-303.

Boelens, P.A., Reeves, R.R., Replogle, W.H., Koenig, H.G. (2012). The effect of prayer on depression and anxiety: maintenance of positive influence one year after prayer intervention. *International Journal of Psychiatry and Medicine* 43 (1): 85-98

Bormann, J. E., Thorp, S. R., Smith, E., Glickman, M., Beck, D., Plumb, D., ... & Herz, L. R. (2018). Individual treatment of posttraumatic stress disorder using mantram repetition: A randomized clinical trial. *American Journal of Psychiatry*, in press.

Chang, B. H., Skinner, K. M., & Boehmer, U. (2001). Religion and mental health among women veterans with sexual assault experience. *The International Journal of Psychiatry in Medicine, 31*(1), 77-95.

Chang, B. H., Skinner, K. M., Zhou, C., & Kazis, L. E. (2003). The relationship between sexual assault, religiosity, and mental health among male veterans. *International Journal of Psychiatry in Medicine, 33*(3), 223-239.

Chen, Y. Y. (2005). Written emotional expression and religion: effects on PTSD symptoms. *The International Journal of Psychiatry in Medicine, 35*(3), 273-286.

Chen, Y. Y., & Contrada, R. J. (2009). Framing written emotional expression from a religious perspective: Effects on depressive symptoms. *The International Journal of Psychiatry in Medicine, 39*(4), 427-438.

Cordova, M. J., Riba, M. B., & Spiegel, D. (2017). Post-traumatic stress disorder and cancer. *The Lancet Psychiatry, 4*(4), 330-338.

CSTH (2014). Durham, North Carolina: Duke University Center for Spirituality, Theology and Health. Retrieved on 7/28/18 from https://spiritualityandhealth.duke.edu/index.php/religious-cbt-study/therapy-manuals).

Currier JM, Holland JM, Drescher KD (2015). Spirituality factors in the prediction of outcomes of PTSD treatment for U.S. military veterans. *Journal of Traumatic Stress* 28(1):57-64.

Davidson, J. R., Weisler, R. H., Butterfield, M. I., Casat, C. D., Connor, K. M., Barnett, S., & van Meter, S. (2003). Mirtazapine vs. placebo in posttraumatic stress disorder: a pilot trial. *Biological Psychiatry, 53*(2), 188-191.

Davis, L. L., Jewell, M. E., Ambrose, S., Farley, J., English, B., Bartolucci, A., & Petty, F. (2004). A placebo-controlled study of nefazodone for the treatment of chronic posttraumatic stress disorder: a preliminary study. *Journal of Clinical Psychopharmacology, 24*(3), 291-297.

Deneys, M. L., & Ahearn, E. P. (2006). Exacerbation of PTSD symptoms with use of duloxetine. *Journal of Clinical Psychiatry, 67*(3), 496-497.

Feder, A., Parides, M. K., Murrough, J. W., Perez, A. M., Morgan, J. E., Saxena, S., ... & Iosifescu, D. (2014). Efficacy of intravenous ketamine for treatment of chronic posttraumatic stress disorder: a randomized clinical trial. *JAMA Psychiatry, 71*(6), 681-688.

Foa, E. B., Chrestman, K. R., & Gilboa-Schechtman, E. (2008). *Prolonged Exposure Therapy for Adolescents with PTSD Emotional Processing of Traumatic Experiences, Therapist Guide*. NY, NY: Oxford University Press.

Fontana, A., Rosenheck, R (2004). Trauma, change in strength of religious faith, and mental health service use among veterans treated for PTSD. *Journal of Nervous and Mental Disease* 192: 579-584.

Frank, J. B., Kosten, T. R., Giller, E. L., & Dan, E. (1988). A randomized clinical trial of phenelzine and imipramine for posttraumatic stress disorder. *American Journal of Psychiatry, 145*(10), 1289-1291.

Fulton, J. J., Calhoun, P. S., Wagner, H. R., Schry, A. R., Hair, L. P., Feeling, N., ... & Beckham, J. C. (2015). The prevalence of posttraumatic stress disorder in Operation Enduring Freedom/Operation Iraqi Freedom (OEF/OIF) Veterans: a meta-analysis. *Journal of Anxiety Disorders, 31*, 98-107.

George, K. C., Kebejian, L., Ruth, L. J., Miller, C. W., & Himelhoch, S. (2016). Meta-analysis of the efficacy and safety of prazosin versus placebo for the treatment of nightmares and sleep disturbances in adults with posttraumatic stress disorder. *Journal of Trauma & Dissociation, 17*(4), 494-510.

Gallup Poll (2017). Religion. Retrieved from https://news.gallup.com/poll/1690/religion.aspx (accessed on 7/28/18)

Gingrich, H. D. (2013). *Restoring the Shattered Self: A Christian Counselor's Guide to Complex Trauma*. Westmont, IL:InterVarsity Press.

Haagen, J. F., Smid, G. E., Knipscheer, J. W., & Kleber, R. J. (2015). The efficacy of recommended treatments for veterans with PTSD: A metaregression analysis. *Clinical Psychology Review, 40*, 184-194.

Harris, J. I., Erbes, C. R., Engdahl, B. E., Thuras, P., Murray-Swank, N., Grace, D., ... & Malec, C. (2011). The effectiveness of a trauma focused spiritually integrated intervention for veterans exposed to trauma. *Journal of Clinical Psychology, 67*(4), 425-438.

Harris, J. I., Usset, T., Voecks, C., Thuras, P., Currier, J., & Erbes, C. (2018). Spiritually integrated care for PTSD: A randomized controlled trial of "Building Spiritual Strength". *Psychiatry Research* 267:420-428.

Hollifield, M., Sinclair-Lian, N., Warner, T. D., & Hammerschlag, R. (2007). Acupuncture for posttraumatic stress disorder: a randomized controlled pilot trial. *Journal of Nervous and Mental Disease, 195*(6), 504-513.

Hopwood, T. L., & Schutte, N. S. (2017). A meta-analytic investigation of the impact of mindfulness-based interventions on post-traumatic stress. *Clinical Psychology Review, 57*, 12-20.

Hoskins, M., Pearce, J., Bethell, A., Dankova, L., Barbui, C., Tol, W. A., ... & Bisson, J. I. (2015). Pharmacotherapy for post-traumatic stress disorder: systematic review and meta-analysis. *British Journal of Psychiatry, 206*(2), 93-100.

IOM Report (2007). Treatment of posttraumatic stress disorder: An assessment of the evidence (Institute of Medicine of the National Academies Report). Washington, DC: The National Academies Press

Kelle, B.E. (2017). Moral injury and the division of spoils after battle in the Hebrew Bible. In McDonald J (ed), *Exploring Moral Injury in Sacred Texts*. London: Jessica Kingsley, pp 83-102

Kessler, R.C., Berglund, P., Delmer, O., Jin, R., Merikangas, K.R., & Walters, E.E. (2005). Lifetime prevalence and age-of-onset distributions of DSM-IV disorders in the National Comorbidity Survey Replication. *Archives of General Psychiatry, 62(6)*: 593-602

Kessler, R. C., Aguilar-Gaxiola, S., Alonso, J., Benjet, C., Bromet, E. J., Cardoso, G., ... & Florescu, S. (2017). Trauma and PTSD in the WHO World Mental Health Surveys. *European Journal of Psychotraumatology, 8*(sup5), 1353383

Koenen, K. C., Ratanatharathorn, A., Ng, L., McLaughlin, K. A., Bromet, E. J., Stein, D. J., ... & Atwoli, L. (2017). Posttraumatic stress disorder in the world mental health surveys. *Psychological Medicine, 47*(13), 2260-2274.

Koenig, H.G. (2016). *You are My Beloved.* Really? CreateSpace: Amazon

Koenig, H.G., Pearce, M.J., Nelson, B., Shaw, S.F., Robins, C.J., Daher, N., Cohen, H.J., Berk, L.S., Belinger, D., Pargament, K.I., Rosmarin, D.H., Vasegh, S., Kristeller, J., Juthani, N., Nies, D., King, M.B. (2015). Religious vs. conventional cognitive-behavioral therapy for major depression in persons with chronic medical illness. *Journal of Nervous and Mental Disease* 203(4): 243-251

Koenig, H. G., Boucher, N. A., Oliver, R. J. P., Youssef, N., Mooney, S. R., Currier, J. M., & Pearce, M. (2017). Rationale for spiritually oriented cognitive processing therapy for moral injury in active duty military and veterans with posttraumatic stress disorder. *Journal of Nervous and Mental Disease* 205(2):147-153.

Koenig, H.G. (2018a). Measuring symptoms of moral injury in Veterans and Active Duty Military with PTSD. *Religions* 9 (3):86 (https://doi:10.3390/rel9030086).

Koenig, H.G. (2018b). *Religion and Mental Health: Research and Clinical Applications.* San Diego, CA: Academic Press (Elsevier)

Koenig, H. G., Youssef, N. A., Ames, D., Oliver, J. P., Teng, E. J., Haynes, K., Erickson ZD, Arnold I, Currier JM, O'Garo K, Pearce M (2018a). Moral injury and religiosity in US Veterans with posttraumatic stress disorder symptoms. *Journal of Nervous and Mental Disease* 206(5):325-331.

Koenig, H.G., Ames D, Youssef N, Oliver JP, Volk F, Teng EJ, Haynes K, Erickson Z, Arnold I, O'Garo KN, Pearce MJ (2018b). Screening for Moral Injury – The Moral Injury Symptom Scale-Military Version Short Form. Military Medicine, in press

Koenig, H.G., Ames, D., Pearce, M.J. (2019). *Religion and Recovery from PTSD.* London, UK: Jessica Kingsley Publishers

Krystal, J. H., Davis, L. L., Neylan, T. C., Raskind, M. A., Schnurr, P. P., Stein, M. B., ... & Huang, G. D. (2017). It is time to address the crisis in the pharmacotherapy of posttraumatic stress disorder: A consensus statement of the PTSD Psychopharmacology Working Group. *Biological Psychiatry, 82*(7), e51-e59.

Kurian, A. G., Currier, J. M., Rojas-Flores, L., Herrera, S., & Foster, J. D. (2016). Meaning, perceived growth, and posttraumatic stress among teachers in El Salvador: Assessing the impact of daily spiritual experiences. *Psychology of Religion and Spirituality, 8*(4), 289-297.

Larson, D. B., Hohmann, A. A., Kessler, L. G., Meador, K. G., Boyd, J. H., & McSherry, E. (1988). The couch and the cloth: The need for linkage. *Psychiatric Services, 39*(10), 1064-1069.

LeBouthillier, D. M., McMillan, K. A., Thibodeau, M. A., & Asmundson, G. J. (2015). Types and number of traumas associated with suicidal ideation and suicide attempts in PTSD: Findings from a US nationally representative sample. *Journal of Traumatic Stress, 28*(3), 183-190.

Lee, D. J., Schnitzlein, C. W., Wolf, J. P., Vythilingam, M., Rasmusson, A. M., & Hoge, C. W. (2016). Psychotherapy versus pharmacotherapy for posttraumatic stress disorder: Systemic review and meta-analyses to determine first-line treatments. *Depression and Anxiety, 33*(9), 792-806.

Lesmana, C. B. J., Suryani, L. K., Jensen, G. D., & Tiliopoulos, N. (2009). A spiritual-hypnosis assisted treatment of children with PTSD after the 2002 Bali terrorist attack. *American Journal of Clinical Hypnosis, 52*(1), 23-34.

Maguen, S., Burkman, K., Madden, E., Dinh, J., Bosch, J., Keyser, J., ... & Neylan, T. C. (2017). Impact of killing in war: A randomized, controlled pilot trial. *Journal of Clinical Psychology, 73*(9), 997-1012.

McIntosh, D. N., Poulin, M. J., Silver, R. C., & Holman, E. A. (2011). The distinct roles of spirituality and religiosity in physical and mental health after collective trauma. *Journal of Behavioral Medicine, 34*(6), 497-507.

NPEC (2016). Northeast Program Evaluation Center: Prescriptions among Veterans with a PTSD diagnosis—Data abstracted from VA Administrative records, June. Washington, DC: VA Office of Mental Health Operations.

O'Garo KG, Koenig HG (2018). A pilot study of Spiritually Integrated Cognitive Processing Therapy in the treatment of moral injury in patients with PTSD. Durham, North Carolina: Duke University Center for Spirituality Theology and Health.

Ori, R., Amos, T., Bergman, H., Soares-Weiser, K., Ipser, J. C., & Stein, D. J. (2015). Augmentation of cognitive and behavioural therapies (CBT) with d-cycloserine for anxiety and related disorders. *The Cochrane Library*. Retrieved on 6-23-18 from http://cochranelibrary-wiley.com/doi/10.1002/14651858.CD007803.pub2/pdf.

Otto, M. W., McHugh, R. K., & Kantak, K. M. (2010). Combined pharmacotherapy and cognitive-behavioral therapy for anxiety disorders: Medication effects, glucocorticoids, and attenuated treatment outcomes. *Clinical Psychology 17*(2), 91-103.

Pargament, K. (2011). *Spiritually Integrated Psychotherapy: Understanding and Addressing the Sacred.* NY, NY: Guildford Press

Pearce MJ, Haynes KN, Currier JM, O'Garo KN, Koenig HG (2017). Religion-Specific SICPT Therapist Appendices. In *Adaptation of CPT: Spiritually-Integrated Cognitive Processing Therapy Veteran/Military Version Therapist's Manual.* Durham, NC: Duke University Center for Spirituality, Theology & Health

Pearce, M.J., Haines, K, Wade, N., & Koenig, H.G. (2018). Spiritually-integrated cognitive processing therapy: A new treatment for PTSD and moral injury. *Global Advances in Health and Medicine 7*, 1-7, https://doi.org/10.1177/2164956118759939

Raskind, M. A., Peskind, E. R., Chow, B., Harris, C., Davis-Karim, A., Holmes, H. A., ... & Romesser, J. (2018). Trial of prazosin for post-traumatic stress disorder in military veterans. *New England Journal of Medicine, 378*(6), 507-517.

Resick PA, Monson CM, Chard KM (2017). *Cognitive Processing Therapy for PTSD.* NY, NY: Guilford Press

Rizzo, A. S., & Shilling, R. (2018). Clinical virtual reality tools to advance the prevention, assessment, and treatment of PTSD. *European Journal of Psychotraumatology 8*(sup5): 1-20

Rogers, D. C. F., & Koenig, H. G. (2013). *Pastoral Care for Posttraumatic Stress Disorder: Healing the Shattered Soul.* London, UK: Routledge (Taylor & Francis)

Rothbaum, B. O., Price, M., Jovanovic, T., Norrholm, S. D., Gerardi, M., Dunlop, B., ... & Ressler, K. J. (2014). A randomized, double-blind evaluation of D-cycloserine or alprazolam combined with virtual reality exposure therapy for posttraumatic stress disorder in Iraq and Afghanistan War veterans. *American Journal of Psychiatry, 171*(6), 640-648.

Sloan, D. M., Marx, B. P., Lee, D. J., & Resick, P. A. (2018). A brief exposure-based treatment versus cognitive processing therapy for posttraumatic stress disorder: A randomized noninferiority clinical trial. *JAMA Psychiatry* 75(3):233-239

Steenkamp, M. M., Litz, B. T., Hoge, C. W., & Marmar, C. R. (2015). Psychotherapy for military-related PTSD: a review of randomized clinical trials. *Journal of the American Medical Association 314*(5), 489-500.

Stein, D. J., Ipser, J., & McAnda, N. (2009). Pharmacotherapy of posttraumatic stress disorder: a review of meta-analyses and treatment guidelines. *CNS Spectrums 14*(1 Suppl 1): 25-31.

Tait R, Currier JM, Harris JI (2016). Prayer coping, disclosure of trauma, and mental health symptoms among recently deployed United States veterans of the Iraq and Afghanistan conflicts. *International Journal for the Psychology of Religion* 26:31-45

VA Research Currents (2018). Retrieved on 6/5/18 from https://www.research.va.gov/currents/0418-Researcher-examines-if-religion-can-ease-guilt-shame-in-Veterans-with-PTSD.cfm

VA/DoD (2017). *VA/DoD Clinical Practice Guidelines for the Management of Posttraumatic Stress Disorder and Acute Stress Disorder*, Version 3.0. Retrieved on 6/7/18 from https://www.healthquality.va.gov/guidelines/MH/ptsd/.

Villarreal, G., Canive, J. M., Calais, L. A., Toney, G., & Smith, A. K. (2010). Duloxetine in military posttraumatic stress disorder. *Psychopharmacology Bulletin*, *43*(3), 26-34.

Volk, F., Koenig, H. G. (2018). Moral injury and religiosity in active duty US military with PTSD symptoms. *Military Behavioral Health* (2018), in press (https://doi.org/10.1080/21635781.2018.1436102)

Wahbeh, H., Shainsky, L., Weaver, A., & Engels-Smith, J. (2017). Shamanic healing for Veterans with PTSD: A case series. *EXPLORE: The Journal of Science and Healing,13*(3), 207- 217.

Walderhaug, E., Kasserman, S., Aikins, D., Vojvoda, D., Nishimura, C., & Neumeister, A. (2010). Effects of duloxetine in treatment-refractory men with posttraumatic stress disorder. *Pharmacopsychiatry*, *43*(02), 45-49.

Watts, B. V., Schnurr, P. P., Mayo, L., Young-Xu, Y., Weeks, W. B., & Friedman, M. J. (2013). Meta-analysis of the efficacy of treatments for posttraumatic stress disorder. *Journal of Clinical Psychiatry* 74(6):e541-e550

Weaver AJ (1995). Has there been a failure to prepare and support Parish-based clergy in their role as front-line community mental health workers? A review. *Journal of Pastoral Care* 49, 129-149

Yehuda R, Bierer LM, Pratchett LC, et al. (2015). Cortisol augmentation of a psychological treatment for warfighters with posttraumatic stress disorder: randomized trial showing improved treatment retention and outcome. *Psychoneuroendocrinology* 51, 589–597.

ABOUT THE AUTHOR

Harold G. Koenig, MD, MHSc, completed his undergraduate education at Stanford University, his medical school training at the University of California at San Francisco, and his geriatric medicine, psychiatry, and biostatistics training at Duke University. He is board certified in general psychiatry, and formerly in family medicine, geriatric medicine, and geriatric psychiatry. He is on the faculty at Duke University Medical Center as Professor of Psychiatry and Associate Professor of Medicine. Dr. Koenig is also an Adjunct Professor in the Department of Medicine at King Abdulaziz University, Jeddah, Saudi Arabia, and in the School of Public Health at Ningxia Medical University, Yinchuan, People's Republic of China, where he teaches and conducts research. Dr. Koenig is the director of Duke's *Center for Spirituality, Theology and Health,* and has published extensively in the fields of religion, spirituality and health, with over 550 scientific peer-reviewed publications and book chapters, and more than 50 books in print or preparation. His research on religion and health has been featured on many national and international TV news programs (including ABC's World News Tonight, The Today Show, two episodes of Good Morning America, Dr. Oz Show, and NBC Nightly News) and hundreds of national and international radio programs and newspapers/magazines (including Reader's Digest, Parade Magazine, Newsweek, Time, and Guidepost). Dr. Koenig has given testimony before the U.S. Senate (1998) and U.S. House of Representatives (2008) concerning the benefits of religion and spirituality on public health.   He is the recipient of the 2012 Oskar Pfister Award from the American Psychiatric Association and the 2013 Gary Collins Award from the American Association of Christian Counselors.

www.ingramcontent.com/pod-product-compliance
Lightning Source LLC
Chambersburg PA
CBHW070031260726
48658CB00002B/592